Praise for BEY

M000015056

Jen Barrick and her mom, Linda, are two women whose faith has been fiercely tested by fire. But deep, painful trials have only made their hearts more tender toward God, as well as to the needs of other women. It's why their insights in the pages of *Beyond Priceless* are so worthy—these two remarkable Christians know of what they write! For any woman who struggles to know God better through testing and trials, this book is a must-read!

JONI EARECKSON TADA
Joni and Friends International Disability Center

Jen's love for God jumps off the pages of this book filled with deep encouragement, hope, and healing. A gift for every woman's heart!

DR. TIM CLINTON
Executive Director of the James Dobson Family Institute
President of the American Association of Christian Counselors

Do you ever struggle with fear of tomorrow? Uncertainties? Do you feel overcome by the many issues in life that leave you doubtful? Jen and Linda Barrick authentically unveil the freedom you can have in Christ as you come to Him just as you are in the book *Beyond Priceless* . A must read for women of all ages seeking to find hope in the midst of the emotional roller coasters experienced in life!

DR. MONICA ROSE BRENNAN
Associate Professor and Director of Women's Ministries,
Christian Leadership and Church Ministries Department,
Liberty University

I don't know about you, but some days, my feelings can get the best of me. What I have found is that naming our feelings is important. Finding the source of our feelings is imperative. But anchoring them in the character of God . . . is life-changing. I only wish I had a resource like this when I was a young woman and aspiring leader. Thank you Jen for this timely reminder of who God is—*Beyond Priceless*.

NOEL BREWER YEATTS
President, World Help

Jen Barrick has such a clear vision of how the Lord truly values each and every one of us. He has all the answers to any insecurities we may experience. In Beyond Priceless, Jen has beautifully woven together a daily devotional that will leave you feeling loved and inspired.

SHARI FALWELL
Senior Pastor's wife, Thomas Road Baptist Church, Lynchburg, VA

Beyond Priceless is exactly that, priceless! This book will capture the heart of young women. It is filled with hope, love, and mercy. Jen has an amazing way to share her feelings and give hope to all. The "When I Feel . . ." statements will leave an impression that will impact girls for the rest of their lives. If young women will learn the lessons from this devotion, it will change their life forever!

MARY COX
Ministers' Wives Consultant / Pastor Wellness,
Georgia Baptist Mission Board; Women's Ministry Director,
North Metro Baptist Church, Lawrenceville, GA

BEYOND

Priceless

WHO GOD IS WHEN I FEEL . . .

JEN BARRICK *WITH* LINDA BARRICK

MOODY PUBLISHERS

CHICAGO

Some details have been changed to protect the privacy of individuals.

All Scripture quotations, unless otherwise indicated, are taken from the Holy Bible, New Living Translation, copyright © 1996, 2004. Used by permission of Tyndale House Publishers, Inc., Wheaton, Illinois 60189, U.S.A. All rights reserved.

Scripture quotations marked (NIV) are taken from the Holy Bible, New International Version®, NIV®. Copyright © 1973, 1978, 1984 by Biblica, Inc.™ Used by permission of Zondervan. All rights reserved worldwide.

Scripture quotations marked ESV are from the ESV® Bible (The Holy Bible, English Standard Version®), copyright © 2001 by Crossway, a publishing ministry of Good News Publishers. Used by permission. All rights reserved.

Scripture quotations marked NASB are taken from the New American Standard Bible®, Copyright © 1960, 1962, 1963, 1968, 1971, 1972, 1973, 1975, 1977, 1995 by The Lockman Foundation. Used by permission. (www.Lockman.org).

Scripture quotations marked GNT are from the Good News Translation in Today's English Version, Second Edition Copyright © 1992 by American Bible Society. Used by permission.

All emphasis in Scripture has been added.

Published in association with the literary agency of Wolgemuth & Associates.

Edited by Annette LaPlaca
Interior and cover design: Erik M. Peterson
Author photo: Leah Stauffer, Gaudium Photography

Library of Congress Cataloging-in-Publication Data

Names: Barrick, Jennifer, author. | Barrick, Linda, author. | Barrick, Jennifer. Priceless.
Title: Beyond priceless : who God is when I feel... / Jen Barrick with Linda Barrick.
Description: Chicago : Moody Publishers, 2020. | Includes bibliographical references. | Summary: "In Priceless: Who I Am When I Feel... Linda and Jen Barrick explore the role feelings play in a woman's spirituality. They now bring you Beyond Priceless: Who God Is When I Feel..., a devotional that invites you to experience the hope and peace God offers in the midst of uncertainty"-- Provided by publisher.
Identifiers: LCCN 2020013634 (print) | LCCN 2020013635 (ebook) | ISBN 9780802419910 (paperback) | ISBN 9780802498847 (ebook)
Subjects: LCSH: Teenage girls--Religious life. | Christian teenagers--Religious life. | Teenage girls--Prayers and devotions. | Christian teenagers--Prayers and devotions. | Spirituality--Christianity--Prayers and devotions. | Emotions--Religious aspects--Christianity--Prayers and devotions.
Classification: LCC BV4551.3 .B37 2020 (print) | LCC BV4551.3 (ebook) | DDC 248.8/33--dc23
LC record available at https://lccn.loc.gov/2020013634
LC ebook record available at https://lccn.loc.gov/2020013635

Originally delivered by fleets of horse-drawn wagons, the affordable paperbacks from D. L. Moody's publishing house resourced the church and served everyday people. Now, after more than 125 years of publishing and ministry, Moody Publishers' mission remains the same—even if our delivery systems have changed a bit. For more information on other books (and resources) created from a biblical perspective, go to www.moodypublishers.com or write to:

Moody Publishers
820 N. LaSalle Boulevard
Chicago, IL 60610

1 3 5 7 9 10 8 6 4 2

Printed in the United States of America

CONTENTS

*To every young woman who has
felt hopeless or unworthy of love*

God is more than enough!

*May you allow Him to capture
your whole heart.*

A NOTE FROM JEN

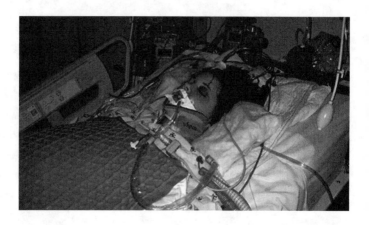

I shouldn't be here. Every EMT on the scene of the accident thought I was dead or would be any moment. At the promising age of fifteen, I was a varsity cheerleader, varsity soccer player, and a straight-A student. I had my whole life ahead of me when a drunk driver ran over my family going eighty miles per hour. It was dark. He wasn't using his headlights. We never even saw him coming.

Our van was smashed beyond recognition. All four of us, including my parents and younger brother, were injured. I suffered a global brain injury, and doctors were

not sure I would ever wake up from a coma. At the scene of the wreck, my level of unconsciousness registered the same as a dead person's.

Word spread quickly. Thousands of people all over the country began praying for me, asking God for a miracle. God had a plan for me far greater than anything I could imagine.

Five weeks later, I began to emerge from the coma, but the real miracle was *how* I woke up. I couldn't sit up or eat. I couldn't walk, and I was almost completely blind at first. I didn't know who my family was, but I knew Jesus! My mind and my body were broken, but the Holy Spirit was alive  and perfect inside of me. Before I could write my name or remember my brother's name, I could pray for hours and carry on a two-way conversation with God. I couldn't repeat three words with a speech therapist, but I could re-cite every Scripture verse and sing every praise song I had ever hidden away in my heart. God's Spirit was whole and active in the midst of my brokenness, and He is still the strongest part of me.

In the years of recovery ahead, my family would suffer more trouble than we ever expected to in this world: multiple surgeries, three cancers, radiation, chronic pain, and endless body scans and blood work. I'm still legally blind and have short-term memory loss. I can't drive a car or focus for more than a few hours without needing to rest. My life will never be the same. I have lots of hidden disabilities, and every day is hard. But I'm not

sad. I'm overflowing with peace and joy because I learned a secret in the midst of my greatest trials: *Jesus is enough!*

Life is hard. You may not have been run over by a

drunk driver, but chances are something has crushed your hopes and dreams. I don't know what you are going through right now, but I do know that Jesus is enough. I want you to know Him like I know Him, to learn to talk to Him all day long like He is standing right beside you, because He is! Jesus is holding your hand. You are never alone.

Can you believe that the God who controls kings and kingdoms, who is beyond our earthly dimension, beyond our comprehension, wants to be with us? God is so majestic and uncontainable that our human minds can't even begin to fathom Him, yet He desires to come close and have an intimate, personal relationship with each one of us that is unique and special. He wants to be everything you need. But for you to receive all that He is, you have to get to know Him better. Maybe you have been hurt or disappointed by the pain of this world. Run to God. He is exactly what you're looking for every moment of every day.

There is so much more to who God is than I ever imagined at the age of fifteen. He is Almighty, yet tender. He knows everything about you and still loves you unconditionally. He's your Counselor, Protector, Defender, Provider, and Best Friend. Time or words can never fully describe Him. During your darkest moments, when you feel completely hopeless, He will put you back together again. You can trust your broken pieces to His hands.

He is good, and He works all things for your good.

A news reporter once asked me if I could go back and undo our wreck, would I do it? I immediately answered, "No, because I would have never known God the way I do now. He is my everything, and He is all I need. He's the reason I get up in the morning!"

Most people think my brain injury is a tragedy. I think it's a blessing, a gift that has led me to know Jesus in a way I may have never known Him. He is *Beyond Priceless*. There is nothing in this world worth more than knowing Him. Philippians 3:8 explains exactly how I feel: "Yes, everything else is worthless when compared with the infinite value of knowing Christ Jesus my Lord. For his sake I have discarded everything else, counting it all as garbage, so that I could gain Christ."

Trading my old life for knowing Jesus was enough is the best thing that ever could have happened to me. I want you to know Him personally the way I know Him. Each page of this devotional was prayed over and designed with you in mind. I cannot write in my own strength, but the Holy Spirit floods my mind and heart with wisdom, and I speak it out loud. My mom records my voice on her iPhone as quickly as she can because I'll never be able to remember how to repeat it the same way! Since my brain is broken, my priorities have changed. I don't care about the things of this world as much. It helps me see Jesus more clearly. I have to rely on Him every moment just to get through the day, so I have really gotten to know Him over the past few years.

My brain injury changed my personality. I used to hide my feelings, but now I don't have as many filters and I say my feelings out loud. Feelings are not bad; they are God-given gifts. They are very real, worthy of validation and expression, but they aren't always true. We have to run to God's Word for truth. It's the one thing that never changes and stays the same. It's like a rock. You can stand on it. God's Word has the power to transform your life.

 My mom and I have organized this thirty-day devotional around the feelings young women experience most often. Let's face it: as we move through adolescence and into young adulthood, we come into contact with a lot of crazy feelings. Each feeling has a root, a place where it began. It's our job to determine if the root is anchored in Christ or not. Feelings will come and go, but the character of God is the same yesterday, today, and forever. The ups and downs of our feelings teach us to understand and experience new attributes of God and learn to rely on Christ, our solid ground.

This is the prayer and desire of my heart. I'm praying this with you in mind. I want you to know God and learn to communicate to Him in a way that maybe you've never known before. Will you pray this prayer with me?

Dear Heavenly Daddy,

Capture my whole heart. I want to go beyond head knowledge and experience You in ways I never dreamed possible. I want to feel the peace of Your presence. My heart wants to go deeper with You and learn more about Your majesty and glory.

Lord, You are beyond anything I could ever ask or imagine. Your wisdom is endless. Your ways are higher than my ways. Your friendship with me is Beyond Priceless. I cannot believe the King of the world wants to communicate with me daily.

Teach me more about who You are. Reveal Yourself to me, Jesus. You are exactly what I need today. I believe the best is yet to come! Amen.

When I feel ordinary . . .
God is BEYOND PRICELESS

 What is the one stand-out quality you think makes you special or different from everyone else? Describe it in writing or draw a sketch of it.

I was sure I was really going places until middle school. Then, suddenly, I became self-conscious about all the things I used to think made me special. I started to deal with the reality that I probably wasn't going to play soccer in college or even get a solo in the choir concert, much less win *American Idol*. No matter how much I dreamed about being amazing or sensational, I felt ordinary.

If you've ever felt ordinary, or if you just now struggled to write down anything you think makes you stand out as special, you are experiencing what most of us experience as we begin to become more aware of ourselves and the world around us. As our world becomes bigger, we feel smaller and less sure of who we are. Believe it or not, that's how God designed it. He perfectly planned the stages of our life so that as we grew up, we would need to press into Him more, and when we did, we would discover how big and wide and deep He is.

God is *Beyond Priceless*! He's beyond my imagination. God is holy. He is majesty. He is love. God is everywhere. He's the air I breathe. I can't fully understand Him, but I can know Him personally and intimately. God is the one true hope of the world. He is my expectation. I rest in His everlasting arms and know I am safe and secure.

Sometimes God lets us run out of our high view of ourselves so we can grasp a higher view of Him, but that does not mean we are ordinary. That just means we are perfectly set up for God to fill us with His love and power and attributes, making us into something extraordinary.

In fact, you can't be ordinary. There is no one like you. Guess what? You are an ORIGINAL! God threw out the mold when He created you. No one else has your same awesome laughter, your personality, your intricate mind. When God handcrafted and designed you, He had eternity in mind. He sees who you will become when You are filled with His Spirit. When He looks at you, He sees the lives you will influence. He has something unique for you to do that will impact eternity. He wants you to seek His name and look to Him for confidence because He has something for your life far bigger and greater than you could ever dream.

During my middle school years, I had another transformation. A youth pastor taught me to start journaling my feelings and hopes and dreams to Jesus. Instead of keeping all of my feelings bottled up inside, I learned to pour them out in a journal and lay them at the feet of Jesus. I can honestly say that learning how to talk to Jesus through writing down questions and feelings is what helped me survive those in-between years and the difficult years that followed my accident. As I interacted with Jesus and read His Word, I started writing down prayers asking to trade my ordinary identity and inadequacies for His extraordinary plan for my life.

JEN'S JOURNAL ENTRY, 2006 (AT AGE FIFTEEN)

Father,

I know You choose the foolish ones, the weak ones, to shame the strong and the wise. God, that means You can take me just as I am (1 Corinthians 1:26–29). You can take me, a nobody, and turn me into a somebody. I know with You all things are possible (Matthew 19:26). Take this year and my life and allow Your glory to shine! Take it and use it to its full potential.

My wildest dreams for my life do not even come close to what God has prepared for me. God doesn't want me to be normal and blend in. I am not ashamed to be different. In all honesty, I want the challenge. The best plans I have for my life will be far exceeded with God's help.

One of the most admired young girls in all of history started out as a typical teenager. Mary, the mother of Jesus, was just a young girl from a low-income family until she was chosen to carry a priceless treasure into the world—Jesus! When the angel appeared to Mary to tell her the news, at first she was confused and afraid. Yet, in the midst of her uncertainty about who she was and whether she was gifted enough for this calling, she surrendered to God's plan. In her surrender, she discovered how great and mighty God is. Look at how she describes Him:

Oh, how my soul praises the Lord.
    How my spirit rejoices in God my Savior!
For he took notice of his lowly servant girl,
    and from now on all generations will call
        me blessed.
For the Mighty One is holy,
    and he has done great things for me.
He shows mercy from generation to
        generation
    to all who fear him.
His mighty arm has done tremendous
        things!

LUKE 1:46–51

God has a special purpose for you just like He had a unique purpose for Mary. You can never be ordinary when you carry Jesus in your heart. You hold the most priceless treasure, the Hope of the world, and God has a plan only you can fulfill to share His love with others. It doesn't matter who you are or what you've done because you are invited to trade your less-than-remarkable qualities for God's extraordinary qualities! My prayer is that in the weeks ahead, you will discover more about who God is and begin to embrace His view of you as your new identity— *Beyond Priceless!*

Dear Great I AM,

I'm not going to lie. Sometimes I feel unseen, unheard, and invisible. Then I realize I can't be ordinary because I have the Holy Spirit, God Himself, living inside me. Wow! Lord, You are Beyond Priceless. I can't even begin to fathom who You are. You spoke the whole world into existence. Reveal to me more of who You are. Let who You are overshadow who I am.

Lord, I come before You with an excited but heavy heart. I don't know what the future holds, but I know I can trust You. What an honor to be chosen by You. Just like Mary, I want to surrender everything to You.

Lord, I give You my available heart. Please use me to do the impossible! Use me to carry the hope of Jesus to the world! Help me reflect a hint of Your glory and carry a hint of Your character. Equip me for the journey through life.

Write your own prayer of expectation to God.

When I feel anxious . . .
God is my PEACE

What circumstances cause you to feel anxious? After my brain injury, I had severe anxiety; I could not walk into a room full of people without shaking. Crowds and noise were overwhelming. I couldn't even go to church or sit in the waiting room at a doctor's office. I had this verse written on a hot pink index card next to my bed, and I would read it every morning:

> Do not be anxious about anything, but in every situation, by prayer and petition, with thanksgiving, present your requests to God. And the peace of God, which transcends all understanding, will guard your hearts and your minds in Christ Jesus.
>
> PHILIPPIANS 4:6–7 NIV

I challenge you to write this passage on a sticky note or index card and put it on your bathroom mirror or somewhere you will see it every day and can claim it out loud.

Dear God,

Life has hardships and trials. I am claiming Your promise that says "Do not be anxious about anything" but pray about everything, and Your peace will guard my heart and mind. I pray Your truth would shine greater and be louder than any other voice I hear. I choose to follow You. I know with Your help, I will be an overcomer. Prince of Peace, I need You. I can't do it alone. Please come to my rescue. I can't wait to see how You will transform my anxiety into something beautiful.

Peace means there is no war, no battle going on in my mind. Peace is stability and stillness of mind. It's what our souls long for. When I am at peace, I am confident, secure, not worried, not trying to defend myself. My brain and body are at ease. It doesn't mean I know what will happen in the future, but I am trusting God. If I give my mind to the Lord, He will renew it and give me His perspective. Peace means I am believing God knows what is best for me and will do what is best for me.

I was diagnosed with thyroid cancer seven years ago, and even though my last body scan indicates that I'm clear of any cancer, I still have a lifelong battle of blood work every six months just to make sure no cancer cells have returned. Even though cancer is out of my control, I can still have peace. I know what happens in the end: God's peace will rule and reign forever!

Not only does God give peace, He *is* peace. Jesus is the Prince of Peace. After Jesus rose from the dead, before He ascended back into heaven, He promised to send the gift of the Holy Spirit. Here is how He describes the Holy Spirit: "I am leaving you with a gift—peace of mind and heart. And the peace I give is a gift the world cannot give. So don't be troubled or afraid" (John 14:27).

Dear Almighty Prince of Peace,

Thank You that I don't have to look for peace like a lost treasure. Scripture says peace is a gift from You. Peace is found and anchored in who I am in You. Thank You for the promise that You will guard my heart and mind. I lift all of my anxious thoughts up to You today. Please shine Your peace over me. Thank You that I am secure in Your almighty hand. I can't stop smiling because Your Holy Spirit lives in me, and I can tap into Your peace any time and any place. Your peace never runs out!

We aren't the author of peace. Peace is a gift from God, and it's renewable every day. God's peace is unlimited. The fruit of the Spirit is love, joy, peace (Galatians 5:22). God's peace is there—you just have to ask for it and receive it. If you are a Christian, peace lives inside you. You can tap into God's peace anytime you need it.

One of my favorite Bible stories tells how Jesus stood up in a boat during a storm on the Sea of Galilee and said, "Peace, be still"—and even the winds and the waves obeyed Him:

> And a great windstorm arose, and the
> waves were breaking into the boat, so that
> the boat was already filling. But he was
> in the stern, asleep on the cushion. And
> they woke him and said to him, "Teacher,
> do you not care that we are perishing?"
> And he awoke and rebuked the wind and
> said to the sea, "Peace! Be still!" And the
> wind ceased, and there was a great calm.
>
> MARK 4:37–39 ESV

Jesus is the highest authority. When I can't control the storm or the situation, I have to trust that God has my best interest in mind and that He will carry me through. You can picture Him rising up in the middle of your stormy circumstance and saying, "Peace! Be still!"

What storm are you in right now?

Ask the Holy Spirit to show you why you are anxious. What lie are you believing about that storm or circumstance?

Journal a prayer asking God to help you replace any lies with His truth.

Sometimes we are too busy to receive peace. It doesn't mean God's not giving it. Peace is everywhere. Just go outside and hear the birds chirp or feel the constant wind on your face. God is everywhere!

Often praise music helps focus all my anxious thoughts on God instead of on my problem.

What things do you like to do to feel peace?

I have learned from my brain therapy sessions that it is important to limit the amount of time we look at our cellphones. Several studies now indicate that our anxiety increases the more we look at our phones. Consider taking up this social-media challenge: take a break from social media for one week, then come back and record if you felt less anxiety during that week.

When I feel broken . . .
God is the GREAT TRANSFORMER

What do you do when something—your favorite coffee mug, flat iron, purse, or bronzer—breaks? Since broken things are worthless because they can't be used, we tend to throw them away and go out to buy a new one. But it's not possible to go shopping for a new brain, body, relationship, or family. So what do you do when *you* are broken? The same thing you do when something valuable, like your car or laptop, quits working. You take it to someone who knows how to fix it.

No matter how broken you are, you never lose your value. God never views you as worthless. When you are broken, He loves you all the more. He will never refuse you or discard you. In fact, He would rather have you come to Him broken than pretending to be anything else. Most of us want something that "looks" like it's new and whole, but that's not how God feels. His Word says He longs to be near the brokenhearted and that He actually prefers us that way:

> The sacrifice you desire is a broken spirit.
> You will not reject a broken and
> repentant heart, O God.

PSALM 51:17

Jesus takes us just as we are, broken and messy. He is the great Transformer. We become a new creation in His hands. He transforms our brokenness into beauty, our pain into purpose, our mess into a new mission. He can't wait to come to our rescue. Our brokenness is often our greatest blessing because it's usually what gets us out of the way and enables the Master to do His greatest work. He longs to change us into something new He can use for His glory.

Friends around you may look as if they have it all together on the outside, but almost everyone is broken somewhere inside. You may wish you could be like someone else, but you don't know what's broken deep beneath their layers of protection. Wholeness is all about perspective. God views wholeness as holiness, righteousness, restoration, things only Jesus can give us *after* we are broken. The world views wholeness as success, health, a perfect body, plenty of followers on social media, or a good-paying job. We get so easily enthralled with celebrities and royalty, what they wear and do and like, but we forget that *we are royalty*! We are daughters of the King. God has the power to transform us, but we have to walk in it, put on the crown, embrace His gifts and His view of us. Embrace the royalty He has to offer, and quit trying to be perfect by the world's standards. Romans 12:2 says, "Don't copy the behavior and customs of this world, but let God transform you into a new person by changing the way you think. Then you will learn to know God's will for you, which is good and pleasing and perfect."

Dear Heavenly Father,

Thank You that I am free to be me. It's an honor to think that I was handpicked by You. Transform my insecurities into a strong tower. Help me not to look at myself in shame or defeat. In You, I am whole; in You, I have victory. I want to embrace that victory and claim it out loud. Thank You for not being a dead king but a Risen King— Almighty Jesus, Savior of the world!

My eyes are broken because my brain is broken. I am legally blind and can't drive . . . *yet* (God just might fix that some day). But do you know what? I'm so grateful for my ears! Because my eyes are broken, my ears are stronger. When one sense is hindered, the others are strengthened. I hear everything with my ears before I see it. The same is true for you. When something inside you is broken, it enables something else to be strengthened. Maybe God had to allow you to go through something hard so He could become stronger in you! When we are completely dependent on God, that's when the impossible happens. God can transform your brokenness into something beautiful and give you purpose.

Read Isaiah 61:1–2 out loud and pray it back to God.

> The Spirit of the Sovereign LORD is upon me,
>   for the LORD has anointed me
>   to bring good news to the poor.
> He has sent me to comfort the
>   brokenhearted
>   and to proclaim that captives will be
>   released
>   and prisoners will be freed.
> He has sent me to tell those who mourn
>   that the time of the LORD's favor has come,
>   and with it, the day of God's anger
>   against their enemies.

Lord Jesus,

*My heart is grateful when I think that You came to
this earth just to set the captives free, to free me!
I can feel the chains falling off. I am whole and
free in You today. Show me how I can replace my
brokenness with the beauty and perfection of
who You are. Daddy, I'm a new creation in You!
It is a privilege to be Your child, Your hand-chosen
daughter, Your princess. Help me never to pick
up those chains again. I want to view myself as
royalty—with no shame, no guilt, no doubt. I am
free! I want to live in Your victory. Thank You for
transforming me and being my One True King.*

That verse you just prayed back to God is followed by a
precious promise of beautiful healing and renewal:

> To all who mourn in Israel,
>   he will give a crown of beauty for ashes,
> a joyous blessing instead of mourning,
>   festive praise instead of despair.
> In their righteousness, they will be like
>   great oaks
>   that the LORD has planted for his own glory.

ISAIAH 61:3

Dear All-sufficient One,

Thank You for taking the time to transform my life. You have changed my physical and emotional scars into something beautiful. Even though I have disabilities and struggle every day, You have REMODELED me and made me better. I promise to no longer look at myself in shame. I know with You the best is yet to come. I praise You in advance for using me in ways I never dreamed possible for Your glory.

Isaiah 61:3 says we will "be like great oaks that the LORD has planted for his own glory." Even big oak trees start as a tiny seed that has to be broken to grow.

 Brokenness comes before growth (strengthening) and before God's glory can be made known. How has this been true in your life?

When I feel defeated . . . God is VICTORIOUS

Have you ever fought a battle in your sleep that seemed so real, but when you woke up, you realized it was all a dream? You weren't actually fighting at all; you were just wrangling with your pillow. I think it will be like that when we get to heaven. We'll realize that all the struggles we faced on earth weren't really us fighting our own battles; it was God fighting for us—and He was winning the whole time. So why in the world should we wear ourselves out fighting or fearing defeat?

Do you ever feel defeated, or like you're losing a battle, in any of these areas?

(Circle the battles you are facing right now.)

School   Work   Relationships   Friendships

Family   Identity   Sports   Confidence

Temptations   Addictions   Purpose

Other_____

The first thing you need to know is that you are never fighting alone. When God was first teaching His people, the children of Israel, who He was and what He could do, He gave them this promise: "For the LORD your God is going with you! He will fight for you against your enemies, and he will give you victory!" (Deuteronomy 20:4).

A few generations after God first gave this promise to His people, their leader King Jehoshaphat found himself feeling defeated. He was being attacked by three armies at the same time and was outnumbered on all sides. King Jehoshaphat cried out to God for help, and this is what God said: "Do not be afraid! Don't be discouraged by this mighty army, for the battle is not yours, but God's . . . You will not even need to fight. Take your positions; then stand still and watch the LORD's victory" (2 Chron. 20:15, 17).

Did you catch that? God says, "The battle is not yours, but God's." We can run to God, stand at His side, and watch God be who He is—*Victorious!* The battle does not belong to us; it's His—and He never loses! We win by running to Him. We fight by taking our position by His side and letting Him fight for us.

Dear Faithful One,

Thank You that I can rest and be protected under the shadow of Your wings. Thank You for being my Defender who fights for me. As I face the problems of today, I want to hold my head up high with confidence. I am victorious because You are victorious! You promise to come to my rescue. You will go before me and make a way through the struggles I face that seem impossible.

Probably the biggest battles we ever have to fight are lies. My biggest enemy tends to be my own mind. It's almost as if I'm drowning myself at times. I'm constantly battling the lies Satan feeds me telling me I'll never get better, I'm not smart enough, or no one will ever like me.

One of my favorite ways to get victory over these lies is a little trick I learned from King Jehoshaphat. He was so confident that God would fight for him that he put praise singers in front of His army. Who sends singers into battle? Jehoshaphat! His weapon of choice was worship music. And guess what happened? You have to read this for yourself:

> At the very moment they began to sing and give praise, the LORD caused the armies of Ammon, Moab, and Mount Seir to start fighting among themselves . . . they began attacking each other. So when the army of Judah arrived at the lookout point in the wilderness, all they saw were dead bodies lying on the ground as far as they could see. Not a single one of the enemy had escaped.
>
> 2 CHRONICLES 20:22-24

I have no doubt that if Jehoshaphat and his army had tried to fight this battle in their own strength, there would have been a much different outcome. They didn't just win, they won *big*! It took them three days to collect all their trophies. They used far more energy praising God and celebrating their victory than they did fighting.

Imagine if we chose to tackle life that way!

When I feel defeated, I can turn it into a positive by praising God in advance for coming to my rescue. When

I choose to praise God in the midst of my battles, that worship helps calm the storm in my heart. It gives me hope. It fills my heart with joy. One of the easiest ways to do this is to sing a song or listen to your favorite worship music! It's almost impossible to feel defeated or have negative thoughts when you are praising God. So when I'm singing, I'm winning!

What is your favorite praise song? Try singing it out loud right now or listen to it on your playlist.

After focusing your praise on God, do you feel any better about those areas that left you feeling defeated today?

If you are a follower of Christ, you have another weapon besides worship music. You have the Holy Spirit living inside of you, who is able to comfort you continuously with His joy and peace: "But you belong to God, my dear children. You have already won a victory over those people, because the Spirit who lives in you is greater than the spirit who lives in the world" (1 John 4:4).

Holy Spirit,

Fill up my heart with Your courage and unexplainable peace. I can face anything with You on my side. Thank You for holding my hand and directing my steps. Help my mind to believe there is always a way out with You. I am an overcomer because You are stronger and greater than any battles I face. Satan is under my feet; he has no power over me except the lies I choose to believe. And I'm believing truth. I'm believing Jesus!

What is your first line of defense when it comes to fighting your battles? Who or what will you send in to fight first?

Try writing your own praise-song lyrics to God. If you are musically challenged like me, try writing down what it means to you that God is victorious.

When I feel depressed . . .
God is RIGHT BESIDE ME

Have you ever felt hopeless or struggled to get out of bed? I have. God has taught me that I can run into His arms when I feel trapped by my emotions. I can choose to "flip flop" my feelings and speak the positive. For example, when I feel hopeless, I can say, "Lord, You are my hope. You are the reason I get up in the morning. I can't wait to see the plans You have for me today."

Recently I had the honor of praying with a young woman who suffered from clinical depression. We surrounded her and prayed for her complete and total healing in Jesus' name. It was a powerful prayer time, but as soon as her friends left the room, a look of fear came over her face. She said, "Tomorrow all my friends are going to call me, and they are going to want to know if I'm better. What am I going to tell them? They've prayed over me several times before, and my depression didn't go away. It makes me feel like a failure when I disappoint them."

My heart went out to her because I have several disabilities from my brain injury. Even though I want God to heal me immediately, it has been a long journey of healing a little more each day. I told her something I've been learning that she could share with her friends, perhaps saying something like this to them: "I'm healing and moving in the right direction. I am not as depressed today as I was yesterday. I'm learning that I need to rest and seek medical care for my depression. And I'm grateful for friends like you who love me."

Her face lit up. "I can do that!" she exclaimed. "That takes so much pressure off."

During my brain therapy sessions, I have learned that our brains need movement to heal and that healing is usually a journey, not an instant destination. Satan wants us to feel trapped and hopeless in our depression or disability. The way we defeat his lie is by declaring out loud that we are on the *move*. We don't have to be healed all at once to experience healing, we just have to be moving in the right direction to have hope for one more day.

Depression is increasing. People of all ages, genders, and races suffer from clinical depression, which is defined as feeling helpless, worthless, and hopeless.

My injury affected my personality. Many friends wanted to help, but they didn't know what to do or what to say. Some stayed away because it was sad to be around the new injured me or difficult to know what to do with me. If you are depressed, chances are, you feel the same way. You aren't the same person you used to be.

Take heart! You are seen and heard and understood by a Friend who sticks closer than a brother (Proverbs 18:24). God understands you when no one else does! He understands you when you don't understand yourself, and He promises never to leave your side. God's Word tells us He is always close enough to reach out, grab us by the hand, and help: "I hold you by your right hand—I, the LORD your God. And I say to you, 'Don't be afraid. I am here to help you'" (Isaiah 41:13).

Dear Comforter,

Please cradle me in Your everlasting arms today and whisper hope to my heart. Help me know that I am never alone because You are walking beside me, holding my hand. Show me how to trust You in the good times and the bad. Thank You for being

my security and my identity. Thank You that my
soul can find rest in You. I don't have to be enough
because You are enough for every problem I face.
I praise You in advance for healing my wounded
heart a little more today. I know You can mend
every broken place and replace all the lies in
my head with Your truth. I refuse to give Satan
power over me. I'm believing You have an amazing
purpose for me and that I am a beautiful,
priceless treasure, loved by You.

Did you know that one of God's mightiest warriors suffered from depression? That's right! Elijah, the great spiritual leader who prayed fire down from heaven and defeated 450 false prophets of Baal, felt hopeless and afraid. After his greatest mountain-top experience, he ran and hid in the wilderness and battled suicidal thoughts.

> Elijah was afraid and fled for his life . . .
> he went on alone into the wilderness,
> traveling all day. He sat down under a
> solitary broom tree and prayed that he
> might die. "I have had enough, LORD,"
> he said. "Take my life, for I am no better
> than my ancestors who have already died."

Then he lay down and slept under the broom tree. But as he was sleeping, an angel touched him and told him, "Get up and eat!" He looked around and there beside his head was some bread baked on hot stones and a jar of water! So he ate and drank and lay down again.

1 KINGS 19:3–6

I love how God sought after Elijah and rescued him at his darkest moment. He didn't condemn Elijah for being depressed. He didn't abandon him for doubting his purpose. Instead, He came close and touched Elijah and brought him food and water.

For a moment, Elijah seemed to forget that God is omnipresent—right beside him in the highs and the lows. God had shown Himself all-powerful by sending fire on Mt. Carmel, but God had to show Elijah personally that He is also present on the bad days. He is with us whether we are winning or losing. Through Elijah's story, we learn that not only is our Creator a God of power, but also a God of compassion and understanding.

God knew exactly what Elijah needed. He didn't leave him stuck alone under the tree in the wilderness. He provided a practical plan to get Elijah moving again in the right direction. Look again at 1 Kings 19 to see what God tells Elijah:

- You aren't alone. There are 7,000 other people just like you who understand what you are going through. (verse 18)

- Get up! (verse 5)

- Eat! Actually, God tells him to eat twice. (verses 5–7)

- I have a plan to get you moving again. (verses 16–17)

What could you do today to start moving in the right direction? You might start with something simple and practical like Elijah: get up, get dressed, take a shower, take a nap, or go for a walk.

Try filling in the blanks in these sentences to begin a new pathway of healing in your brain.

I am no longer going to believe the lie that

_____

(I'm alone, I'm not enough, I'm unloved, I'm hopeless, I'm controlled by fear, depression, eating disorder or addiction, etc.)

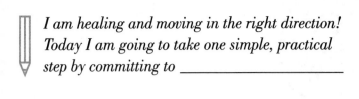

*I am healing and moving in the right direction!
Today I am going to take one simple, practical
step by committing to* _____

_____

(eat, get out of bed, fix my hair, take a shower, go on a
walk, call a friend, read the Bible, take a nap, etc.)

List the things you are learning.

List at least three things you are grateful for.

When I feel empty . . .
God is ALIVE

Have you ever experienced the life-changing power of a Girl Scout cookie? Seriously, you could be missing your one true love until you try one.

Which one is your cookie crush?

☐ Thin Mint

☐ Tagalong

☐ Shortbread

☐ Samoa

☐ Other_____

My grandmother is in love with Samoa Girl Scout cookies. She always has a box of them open in her pantry. If you go searching for one and find an empty box, never fear, there are more boxes stashed in her basement. One time, my little cousin was distraught because he thought Grammy had run out of cookies. I assured him that Grammy never runs out; he was just looking in the wrong place. Then we sneaked to the basement together to grab another box.

Whenever you feel empty, chances are, you are just looking in the wrong place. Maybe you are looking at your circumstances, looking at yourself and your inadequacies, or looking at other people who seem to have everything you don't. The truth is that, as Christians, we are *never* empty. We are filled. The Holy Spirit has a permanent residence in us. He is alive and active, filling us with a never-ending supply of strength, hope, love, courage, contentment, joy, and peace each and every day. These gifts never run out!

Your feeling empty doesn't mean God is no longer there. Your feeling empty doesn't mean God is dead or indifferent to you. That feeling is just a gauge, like the "E" symbol on your gas tank reminding you that it's time to refuel. It's time for you to quit looking in the wrong places and start looking to Jesus, the Author and Perfecter of your faith. Ask Him to fill you with His love, joy, and peace today.

After Jesus died on the cross, His followers were devastated. They thought He was still dead. They, too, went looking in the wrong place to fill their void. They went to the tomb where Jesus had been buried, but it was empty. This is what they saw and heard the angel say:

> "He isn't here! He is risen from the dead, just as he said would happen. Come, see where his body was lying. And now, go quickly and tell his disciples that he has risen from the dead, and he is going ahead of you to Galilee. You will see him there."

MATTHEW 28:6–7

Check out this life-changing promise: The angel invites the women into the empty place, the tomb. Then he says, "Now, go quickly!" He warns them not to stay in the empty place, but to leave their emptiness behind and go looking for Jesus. Why? Because Jesus was *alive*, and they were looking in the wrong place. There was no need to stay in the empty place. The angel gives them this secure and amazing promise if they leave to search for Jesus: you will see Him!

If you are in an empty place today or an empty season of your life, don't despair. Thank God for your emptiness because it can create a longing to be filled. The emptiness is meant to send you searching. The emptiness is meant to help you find your way back to Jesus. And guess what? If you go looking for Him, *you will see Him*. That's a promise you can count on, now and for eternity: "If you look for me wholeheartedly, you will find me" (Jeremiah 29:13).

Lord Jesus,

Thank You for placing in all of our hearts that desire NOT to be satisfied but seek for more, to ask for more, to live with more in mind— because there is more in our future, and that is heaven. I can't wait to thank You and praise You one day, face to face. Wow, Jesus, I can't stop smiling. I can't wait to see You!

You don't have to stay in your empty place, and you don't have to wait for heaven to feel better because I have some more mind-blowing news for you today. This will change the way you get out of bed in the morning:

> The Spirit of God, who raised Jesus from the dead, lives in you. And just as God raised Christ Jesus from the dead, he will give life to your mortal bodies by this same Spirit living within you.

ROMANS 8:11

The same power that raised Jesus from the dead lives in you! What does this mean to you?

How does this truth change your day today and your tomorrow?

Is the way you're living your life evidence that Jesus is alive?

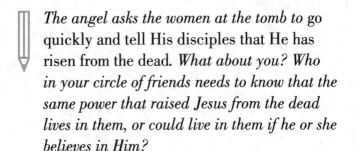

The angel asks the women at the tomb to go quickly and tell His disciples that He has risen from the dead. *What about you? Who in your circle of friends needs to know that the same power that raised Jesus from the dead lives in them, or could live in them if he or she believes in Him?*

Who do you need to tell about Jesus? Write his/her name.

_____

God is ALIVE

Risen Savior,

Thank You for being my best friend, my everything, the reason I get up in the morning. Thank You for filling me with Your dreams and hope for the future. Thank You for believing in me and equipping me to do the impossible. Thank You that You are alive and I can talk to You any time and any place. You hear me and You answer me.

Lord, You want us to find joy and abundance in life through You. No matter what we are going through, we can be filled with the fruit of the Spirit: love, joy, peace, patience, kindness, goodness, faithfulness, gentleness, and self-control (Galatians 5:22–23). Fill me today so I can go and tell someone else about You. You are alive and active in me!

Look in the mirror and repeat this truth out loud:

- **The only thing empty is the tomb.**

- **The same power that raised Jesus from the dead lives in me!**

Now go quickly and tell someone else!

When I feel exhausted . . . God is my REST

Raise your hand if you're exhausted today. Have you ever stopped long enough to ask why? Often when I'm exhausted, I'm putting too much pressure on myself or have too many expectations of what I should be achieving. Sometimes I'm doing lots of good things, but I struggle to say no to the things God prepared for someone else to carry, and I get burned out.

Life isn't a sprint; it's a marathon. God set a pace for us. He created rest. After six days of speaking the world into existence, God rested the entire seventh day. In fact, Sabbath rest is one of the Ten Commandments. Why? Because God knows how much our physical and emotional selves need rest. The command to rest is for our good. We were created in His image, which means that we were created to enjoy regular rhythms of rest just like He did.

Often the more we have on our to-do list, the more we forget *to do* the most important thing, which is to spend time with God. God's presence is a place of rest; it's a break from the world and its burdens. Feed your soul with God's love letter. Seek Him every day. God's Word reveals His beauty and His purpose for our lives. The more we read it, the more we experience God as our rest and renewal. Jesus said, "Come to me, all of you who are weary and carry heavy burdens, and I will give you rest. Take my yoke upon you. Let me teach you, because I am humble and gentle at heart, and you will find rest for your souls. For my yoke is easy to bear, and the burden I give you is light" (Matthew 11:28–30).

Almighty Great I AM,

I run to You today, a place of safety and security that nothing can pass through. When I look into Your eyes through Your Word, everything else vanishes because I know I am right where I'm meant to be. Please renew my mind and soul today. You are my strength, my security, and my safe haven. I want to rest right here. I don't want to move. I want my heart to be captured by Your warm embrace.

Jesus said His yoke is *easy* and His burden is *light*. If your life seems exhausting, maybe you are trying to do things in your own strength. We get lost in our own pressures. We try to make God fit into our agenda, when we need to sit at His feet and let Him dictate our agenda. It saves us a lot of time and frustration when God gives us His plans for the day before we start running. If God is in it, nothing can stop it. If God isn't in it, we are wasting our energy.

What heavy burdens do you want to let go of today and give to Jesus?

Ask the Holy Spirit right now to show you what tasks you are trying to do in your own strength. Can you visualize yourself handing those tasks to Jesus to hold?

God can't wait to meet with you and listen to you. Have you ever thought that God even wants to share in your joy and laughter? I bet that is exactly what your soul needs. We were created to have a relationship with God. When we forget to spend time with Him, our soul craves it. We have more joy when we do less and spend more time in God's presence. When we rest in His presence, He will revive us.

What is your favorite way to spend time with God and experience His presence?

☐ Journaling your thoughts and prayers

☐ Dancing to praise music

☐ Singing a worship song

☐ Walking and enjoying His presence in nature

☐ Reading His Word, which is His love letter to you

☐ Listening to your favorite preacher on a podcast

☐ Painting a picture of His creation

☐ Other _____

God is always talking, but we aren't always listening. Take time to just rest and talk to Him and ask Him your questions, then journal what He speaks to your heart or the Scripture He brings to your mind. It's okay to give your mind and heart permission to rest or even to take a nap. You can rest knowing God is in control of everything. Did you know that when we rest we create a posture of trust? I don't have to be enough or do more because God is enough!

You can rest in God's faithfulness. Describe a time when God was faithful to you.

You can rest in God's promises. What is your favorite promise in Scripture?

One of my favorite promises is found in Psalm 91:1–2:

> Those who live in the shelter of the Most High
>   will find rest in the shadow of the Almighty.
> This I declare about the LORD:
> He alone is my refuge, my place of safety;
>   he is my God, and I trust him.

God is my REST

Dear Gracious Father,

Not only do I love the visual image of resting in the shadow of Your almighty wings, but it helps me remember that You are my protection and my safe haven. I want to rest in You. I know my soul needs rest. I know rest keeps me healthy. Not only do I want to "go" for You, but I want to rest in Your arms and find my strength again in You. Help me to seek you and find You like hidden treasure. Just being with You is my reward.

I love You, Daddy!

Jesus is our example. He modeled rest before His day began and at the end of His day. Both Matthew and Mark describe Jesus taking time out:

> After sending them home, he went up into the hills by himself to pray. Night fell while he was there alone.
>
> **MATTHEW 14:23**

> Before daybreak the next morning, Jesus got up and went out to an isolated place to pray.
>
> **MARK 1:35**

Jesus, Jesus, Jesus,

I'm just grinning from ear to ear. Thank You for the gift of rest. You modeled rest through Scripture. When You were exhausted from the crowds of people, You got alone to pray and connect with Your Father. If You needed time to rest and recharge and plug into Your Power Source, how much more do I need to get away from the confusion and truly rest?

What is one thing you could do today to rest?

When I feel financial stress . . . God is my PROVIDER

A couple of hours before our car wreck I was singing these words with my high school choir: "His eye is on the sparrow and I know He watches." Five weeks later when I started to wake up from a coma, I was still mouthing those same song lyrics. My parents were in their wheelchairs with tears streaming down their faces as they watched me sing with joy and total dependence on my heavenly Daddy to provide my every need. My brain was so injured I didn't know I was hurt. I couldn't walk or eat or sit up by myself, but I was singing words that were speaking truth to my parents. They didn't know how they were going to pay our catastrophic hospital bills or how they would take care of me. They were just trying to survive one day at a time. I can tell you this: God has met our every need. He is faithful one day at a time. That doesn't mean it has been easy. When you go through a stressful financial time, He is your Provider. And guess what? His provision never runs out!

The song I was singing comes from this passage of God's Word: "What is the price of two sparrows—one copper coin? But not a single sparrow can fall to the ground without your Father knowing it. And the very hairs on your head are all numbered. So don't be afraid; you are more valuable to God than a whole flock of sparrows" (Matthew 10:29–31).

When I feel financial stress, I'm looking at my limited resources instead of at God's *unlimited* riches. I've learned that if I turn my "begging" into "praising" it makes me feel better. It gives me hope. As I focus on who God is, my problems begin to feel smaller.

List two financial needs you have right now.

1. _____

_____

2. _____

_____

God is good, and He is always faithful, even when He answers our prayers in a way we don't expect. And God is not earthbound, which means we can't begin to fathom His resources. He can do more than is humanly possible.

Write a prayer about your two financial needs, praising God for being your Provider.

God promises to provide for our needs. Notice three things this passage tells us about God as our Provider.

> So don't worry about these things, saying, "What will we eat? What will we drink? What will we wear?" These things dominate the thoughts of unbelievers, but your heavenly Father already knows all

your needs. Seek the Kingdom of God
above all else, and live righteously, and
he will give you everything you need.

MATTHEW 6:31–33

Did you see the three things? First, your heavenly Father already knows what you need *before* you ask! Second, we are commanded to seek God's kingdom first. And third, God will give you everything you need (not everything you want or even everything you think you need, but this is a promise that God, who loves you so much, will give you exactly what you need).

What does it mean to seek God's kingdom first? One way we seek the kingdom first is with our money. My parents always taught me the importance of giving a portion of my money to God first before I spent any of it. When we give to God first, He promises not only to provide for our needs but to bless us over and above what we entrusted to Him. The more I give to God, the more I see His miraculous provision: "Give, and it will be given to you. A good measure, pressed down, shaken together and running over, will be poured into your lap. For with the measure you use, it will be measured to you" (Luke 6:38 NIV).

Another thing that happens when I give to God first is that it helps my heart to be focused on the things of God. It helps me be less selfish. Let's face it, no matter how many clothes, makeup, shoes, jewelry, or cars we buy, we always want more. We always want what we don't have. The more we have, the more we want or think we need. The opposite happens when we give. The more we give, the more content and joyful we are. Our hearts follow our money trail: "Wherever your treasure is, there the desires of your heart will also be" (Matthew 6:21).

The more money I spend on something, the more I give my heart to it, the more valuable it becomes to me. So the more money I give back to God, the more He has my heart and attention, and the more I get to know Him as my Provider. Money can easily become either a destructive cycle that cannot be quenched, or a continuous cycle of overflowing joy that leads to more peace and contentment.

What if we turned our focus from what we need to what we can give? What if whenever we wish we could buy something, instead we look around to see what we have in excess that we could give away? Maybe you have three coats, and you could give one to someone who has none. Maybe you have fifteen pairs of shoes and you could give four pairs away. Maybe you have a drawer full of makeup you aren't using. Maybe you have a car and know some-one who isn't able to drive and needs a ride. Perhaps you know someone who needs food and you could make them a meal or give them an anonymous gift card to the grocery store. You could be someone else's *miracle*! You could become a part of God's provision for someone else.

What three things do you have in your closet that you could give away?

1. _____

2. _____

3. _____

List three acts of kindness you could do for someone else.

1. _____

2. _____

3. _____

I'm smiling right now because I know just by making that list your heart is feeling more joy and less stress. Give what you have in your hand to God and trust Him to give back everything you really need. He either is the King of the world or He's not. Who does your giving say He is?

Dear King of All Things,

You are my Strength and my Provider. The earth is Yours and everything in it. How could I ever not trust You to take care of me? I don't really have the ability to provide for my own financial needs right now, but You do. I trust You, Almighty Father. While I'm waiting for You to provide, show me something I already have in my hand that You want me to give to You or someone You love. What can I give to You today? Lead me to trust You and see Your provision beyond what is humanly possible.

When I feel forgotten . . . God is my EVERLASTING FATHER

There's almost nothing worse than feeling unseen or unheard. We each have an innate human desire to belong. Just like we need food and water, we need a place to belong. As you navigate through some of life's biggest transitions—becoming a teen and then a young adult—you will have to find a sense of belonging, even in new places and uncharted waters. You might find yourself in situations where you feel forgotten. Be assured: *You are never forgotten!*

God's Word tells us He is constantly thinking about us, even when we are asleep! We can't even begin to count the number of times we are on His mind and heart:

How precious are your thoughts about me,
O God.
They cannot be numbered!
I can't even count them;
they outnumber the grains of sand!
And when I wake up,
you are still with me!

PSALM 139:17–18

Depending on your experiences and life situation, the word *God* might seem far away and untouchable to you. Maybe you feel like you aren't good enough to approach Him. Maybe you never learned how to draw near to Him. Maybe you feel like God has better things to do than to care about you. Or maybe you feel disappointed because you think He chose not to intervene for you.

God's own chosen people the Israelites must have felt forgotten by God. Before Jesus came to earth as a baby, they had not heard from God in four hundred years! (That's how much time passed between the Old Testament and New Testament in the Bible.) Imagine if someone didn't message you back in four minutes, much less four hundred years. The Israelites also were not allowed to write or speak the name of God because it was considered so holy. Only the high priest could enter God's presence in the Most Holy Place in the temple (Exodus 26:33). The average person had to wait outside that special place. Don't get me wrong: God is indeed so much higher and holier than we could ever imagine! My point is that until Jesus came to die for us, many people never really experienced a personal, intimate relationship with God.

Jesus came into a world of people who felt forgotten. He came to give us a gift that would solve our need to belong forever. He came to make us part of His family. In two words Jesus changed the way that we would relate and communicate with God forever. Jesus' followers asked Him to teach them how to talk to God. And here is what Jesus said that would forever give us a place to belong: "Pray like this: Our Father in heaven, may your name be kept holy" (Matthew 6:9).

Did you catch those two words? *Our Father.* He could have said, "My Father" (as in mine, not yours). He could have said, "O Holy Untouchable God, whose name you are not allowed to speak," but He didn't. In two words He invited us to become part of His family. He specifically chose to include us when He said, "Our Father." Jesus came to make a way for us to become adopted into His family. He came to give us an Everlasting Father! "And he will be called: Wonderful Counselor, Mighty God, Everlasting Father, Prince of Peace" (Isaiah 9:6).

What does the idea of an "Everlasting Father" mean to you?

Jesus made a way for us to be adopted into His family and have His Father be our Father. When you believe Jesus died on the cross for you and ask Him to forgive you of your sins, not only do you get a fresh start, but you get new family. Salvation is by God's grace through faith in what Jesus has done for you on the cross. If you have never become part of God's family, you can pray and receive Him as your Savior right now. Paul explains it this way: "If you openly declare that Jesus is Lord and believe in your heart that God raised him from the dead, you will be saved" (Romans 10:9).

Here's a suggested prayer. It's not the exact words that save you—it's Jesus who saves you, by His death on the cross and His resurrection. But you can receive salvation by turning away from your sins, with a heart attitude of faith and a desire to live for God and follow Him. Take a moment to pray in your own words from your heart to God.

Dear God,

I know I'm not perfect. I need You to forgive me of my sins and save me. I believe You sent Your Son, Jesus, to earth to die for me. I believe You raised Jesus from the dead. Come into my heart and give me new life. I want to live forever with You in heaven. Help me to follow You in everything I say and do. Thank You for making me a part of Your family! Amen!

God's Word explains salvation this way: it's a family relationship! "So you have not received a spirit that makes you fearful slaves. Instead, you received God's Spirit when he adopted you as his own children. Now we call him, 'Abba, Father'" (Romans 8:15).

Abba, Father!

You see me. You chose me as Your daughter. You delight in me. No one can take me out of Your grip. I am Your daughter forever. I'm adopted by You. I'm secure in Your family—the family of God. No matter what happens to me on this earth, no one can take away my relationship with You. I am Yours forever.

Some people translate *Abba* as *Daddy*. The word *Daddy* technically did not exist in the Greek language, but *Abba* suggests personal, affectionate intimacy, and *Daddy* gets close to the idea. I love to use the word *Daddy* when I pray because it makes my heavenly Father feel more personal to me. It makes me feel like I can run to Him and crawl into His lap. I can expect Him to catch me when I fall. I can tell Him everything, and He won't look down on me. I can trust my heavenly Daddy.

Dear Everlasting Father,

I'm beyond grateful for the confidence of knowing I am never forgotten. I am wanted and loved by You, the eternal King. Thank You that I can call You "Daddy." I can trust You to hold me and protect me. As Your daughter I have the hope of heaven and what is to come someday. Ahhh! I can take a deep breath because I am safe in Your arms. I don't know what my day will hold, but I know You hold my future. I know that with You the best is yet to come. Thank You that I am never overlooked by You.

Try writing your own prayer to your heavenly Daddy. What do you want to say to Him today? He wants to have a personal, intimate relationship with you.

When I feel doubtful . . .
God is FAITHFUL

I'm about to ask you some very tough questions. Be completely open and honest: Have you ever doubted God? Do you think it is wrong to doubt God? Why or why not?

For many believers, doubt is a part of our spiritual journey. Some doubts are caused by other influences, some are caused by unimaginable circumstances, and some are just pure curiosity. I might doubt God's love for me, His goodness, or His power. I might doubt that I am who He says I am. I might doubt that His Word is true or that the stories in the Bible actually happened. I might doubt that God sees me, hears me, or forgives my sins. The list can go on and on. Whatever your doubts about God may be, I'm going to ask you to cling to one truth about who God is while you work through your tough questions: "If we are unfaithful, he remains faithful, for he cannot deny who he is" (2 Timothy 2:13).

God is faithful. He cannot be anything else. He is faithful in love and kindness. He is faithful to pursue you. He is faithful even when you can't be. That means you can run to Him with your doubts and questions. Be honest with Him. Many turn away from God because they are doubting and they are not honest with God or don't seek Him for answers. Remember, nothing can separate you from God's love. Your doubts do not make Him love you any less. He is not afraid of your tough questions. He can't wait to spend time with you and listen to what you have to say. He values you. He knows your inner anxious thoughts, so you can be real and vulnerable with Him. Tell Him you are struggling. Ask for help in your unbelief.

Not only does God promise to be faithful, but He also promises to be merciful when we have questions about Him. He commanded His followers to "show mercy to those whose faith is wavering" (Jude 22). Mercy means that you do not get what you deserve. Remember when Jesus rose from the dead and how Thomas doubted it was really Jesus (John 20:25)? Notice how kind and patient Jesus was with Thomas. Then there was also Peter, who rejected and denied even knowing Jesus, just a few hours before He died. After His resurrection, Jesus sought out

Peter to show His love and forgiveness to Him (see John 21). That is the heart of Jesus for you today in the midst of your doubts and questions.

Dear Lover of my Soul,

Thank You for inviting me to come closer and to spend time with You. I'm speechless because there is nothing that I can do to make You stop loving me. I can rest in Your everlasting arms while I grow and wrestle with my faith. You see my potential and what I will become with Your help. Lord, I wish there was a word greater than faithfulness because You go beyond faithfulness.

Would you be willing to answer a few questions? First of all, have you ever considered doubting your doubts? If doubting our faith is a normal part of our spiritual journey, why not doubt our doubts as well? When I doubt God, I am still choosing to put faith in something. I might be trusting myself over God or my friends over God. I might be choosing to believe what the internet says or a social media post over what a holy, omnipotent God says. Belief and doubt both require faith in something. So if I'm going to ask tough questions about God, I should ask the same tough questions about my doubts.

Who am I choosing to trust? Who or what is worthy of my belief? Is it changing or will it last forever?

Secondly, do you really want to believe in a God you can fully explain? Perhaps, you should consider getting comfortable with the idea that some of the mysteries of God will never be explained or revealed this side of heaven. Often when we doubt, we are predominantly trying to humanize God. That means we're trying to understand Him with our limited human minds and emotions. God is supernatural. He is not of our same dimension. We can't sum Him up in words. We can know Him intimately, but we can't fully comprehend and fathom the whole magnitude of who He is. Our minds cannot begin to contain Him:

> "My thoughts are nothing like your
> thoughts," says the LORD.
> "And my ways are far beyond anything
> you could imagine.
> For just as the heavens are higher than
> the earth,
> so my ways are higher than your ways
> and my thoughts higher than your
> thoughts."

ISAIAH 55:8-9

So, do you really want to believe in a God that you can easily explain? When you need a miracle, I bet you'll want a God that is bigger than your ability to fathom. If I could fully explain God to you, I wouldn't be alive today. When my family's van was hit by a drunk driver, I needed a God who could transcend modern medicine and human possibility. I needed a God of miracles! Everyone thought I was dead at the scene of the accident. The rescue workers who carried my body thought there was no hope for me. But God who is far greater than any human could ever comprehend did what no doctor or rescue worker thought was possible. He was strong and powerful inside of me. When my body and mind were broken, He kept me alive and began healing me. When I woke from the coma, I did not recognize my family at first, but I still knew Jesus. That's a God I can't explain, but one that I am willing to trust because He was faithful to me. He stayed right beside me. He was so real to me in those hours of pain, no one will ever be able to get me to deny Him.

What is one doubt you are struggling with right now? Would you be willing to get honest with God and others about your doubt? Consider these last few thoughts before you go on with your day:

1. **God knows what you are thinking, so you might as well be honest with Him. Talk to Him about your doubts and ask Him to reveal His truth to you.**

2. You aren't the first or only person who felt this way. Seek out a safe, trustworthy person (a family member, church leader, or Christian counselor) to help you walk through your tough questions together.

3. Doubts have the potential to weaken your faith or strengthen your faith when you seek God for the answers, so doing #1 and #2 are really important!

When I feel hopeless . . .
God is GOOD

 Based on your current circumstances and the way you feel right now, answer the following questions:

Do you believe God is good?

Has God been good to you?

Can you trust Him?

If you answered no to any of those questions, you might be dealing with some pretty tough stuff. Difficult seasons of illness, financial trouble, break-ups, or disappointments really leave us with two options: We can feel hopeless about our impossible situation, or we can have hope that

God is about to do the impossible despite our situation.

When I feel hopeless, I am putting my circumstances above God and choosing to believe He is not good and not in sovereign control. What I'm really doing is taking God out of the equation when He *is* the equation. He is everything I need plus more. He is the way, the truth, and the life (John 14:6). He is the source of all hope, and He is good.

After our accident, our family experienced seasons of hopelessness. Would we ever walk again, do normal things as a family again, have the ability to pay our bills, wake up without feeling pain? Whenever we started to spiral downward, we clung to this verse that would later become the motto of our ministry, Hope Out Loud: "I pray that God, the source of hope, will fill you completely with joy and peace because you trust in him. Then you will overflow with confident hope through the power of the Holy Spirit" (Romans 15:13).

Hope doesn't come from us or our circumstances. It comes from God. He is the source of all hope, and His supernatural power enables us to "overflow with confident hope" even in the worst of circumstances. There were times when our family started to question *why* God would allow something so painful to happen to us. What we were really asking was: Is God good? Some days we wondered if things would never be good again until we got to heaven, but that is not what God's Word says, so we chose to cling to His Word: "Yet I am confident I will see the LORD's goodness while I am here in the land of the living" (Psalm 27:13).

God is good all the time—not just in heaven, but on earth, not just in the good times, but in the bad. I remember the day God made a story in His Word become very personal for me. It helped me understand why God had allowed something horrible to happen to me. I was reading the story of Shadrach, Meshach, and Abednego in the fiery furnace when I noticed a detail I had never seen before.

These three guys were stuck in a pretty impossible situation. They were kidnapped from their homes and living in captivity in a foreign country under the rule of a crazy narcissist, King Nebuchadnezzar. The king had built a giant gold statue of himself and commanded everyone to worship his statue or be thrown into a fiery furnace as punishment. Shadrach, Meshach, and Abednego were from Israel and worshiped only the One True God. They refused to bow to the king's statue, which enraged King Nebuchadnezzar. He ordered that the furnace be heated seven times hotter than usual, so hot that even the guards who opened the door to the furnace were burned alive without ever falling into the fire!

If you were reading this story for the very first time, or if you were Shadrach, Meshach, and Abednego being dangled over the fire, you'd probably think this situation was hopeless. You'd probably be rooting for someone to come to their rescue and stop them from falling into the fire. But that's not what God did. He did something greater:

> So Shadrach, Meshach, and Abednego, securely tied, fell into the roaring flames. . . .
>
> "Look!" Nebuchadnezzar shouted. "I see four men, unbound, walking around in the fire unharmed! And the fourth looks like a god!"
>
> Then Nebuchadnezzar came as close as he could to the door of the flaming furnace and shouted: "Shadrach, Meshach, and Abednego, servants of the Most High God, come out! Come here!"
>
> So Shadrach, Meshach, and Abednego stepped out of the fire. Then the high officers, officials, governors, and advisers crowded around them and saw that the

fire had not touched them. Not a hair on their heads was singed, and their clothing was not scorched. They didn't even smell of smoke!

DANIEL 3:23–27

It was that sentence that got me, with its detail and reality: "They didn't even smell of smoke!" See, it would have been a really cool miracle if God had kept these obedient men out of the furnace in the first place. But the greater miracle was that God Himself was with them in the furnace! When they came out, they didn't even smell like smoke! Their hair wasn't even singed! When you read the rest of Daniel 3, you'll find out that the whole kingdom heard about God and His almighty power because of this miracle.

As I read this story again, suddenly my life made more sense to me. God could have stopped my accident from happening, but the greater miracle was for God to be with me every day and use my story to help other people. What's my greater miracle? To have a brain injury and be excited about God choosing me for His glory. Sparing us from hard times would be great, but getting us through them with hope is *beyond* great!

The next time you are facing an impossible situation, buckle up. It might be an opportunity for God to do the impossible, to display His power and hope through you.

Lord of Heaven and Earth,

Your goodness is so deep that my mind can't comprehend it. It shines everywhere through all of creation. The birds never stop chirping and praising You because You take care of them. I feel Your goodness in the wind across my face. It's like You're breathing on us, reminding us You're there even when we cannot see You. The seasons shout Your glory. You are good because You are slow to anger. You don't wish anyone to perish, but all to come to repentance. That's why You are slow to fix all the evil in this world, to give everyone a chance to find You.

And You promise to work everything out for my good. Thank You for using me to shout Your love to others. Help me to remember the truth that You are good no matter what circumstances I face. I want to shout Your praise one more time. Thank You for being so good to me!

How might your difficult circumstances be an opportunity for someone to see who God is?

 If just one person had their eternity changed forever because of your story, would your troubles be worthwhile?

 Can God be good even when your circumstances are not?

 Now that you have a different perspective, try answering these questions again:

Is God good?

Has He been good to you?

Can you trust Him?

When I feel inadequate . . . God is **ALL-POWERFUL**

Have you ever felt like you weren't good enough, smart enough, thin enough, ready for a test, or equipped for a job? Maybe you just felt like you were weak from carrying a heavy burden. Perhaps you were taught that you couldn't be weak but had to be tough and push through any problem because weakness was "not an option."

 Describe a time when you felt weak or inadequate.

Who told you that you were not enough?

Ask God to show you when you first started identifying with the words of being less than or inadequate. Then ask the Holy Spirit to reveal to you any lies you started believing about yourself.

You might be surprised to hear that feeling or being inadequate is a blessing in disguise. It sets the stage for you to experience God's power more fully and intimately. Almost always when God calls us to do something, we feel inadequate or incapable of doing it in our own strength. We have to rely on God's power, and that's exactly where God wants us to be, totally dependent on Him. That's when the supernatural happens!

This might shock you. The apostle Paul, one of the most influential people in spreading the gospel besides Jesus Himself, boasted about his weakness! The apostle Paul wrote most of the New Testament, he preached the gospel to the Jews and Gentiles, he even healed people, but Paul struggled when the Lord didn't take away a problem he had. Paul probably often struggled with feeling inadequate. Paul said he had a "thorn in the flesh," and he begged God to remove it. We're not sure what that thorn was exactly, but God refused to remove it because He had something far greater for Paul to experience— the miraculous power of God enabling Him to do the impossible every day. I have thought about this story many times because of my own pain and disabilities. Can you imagine how Paul must have felt? God gave him the power to heal others, but for his own healing, God said "no."

> Three different times I begged the Lord to take it away. Each time he said, "My grace is all you need. My power works best in weakness." So now I am glad to boast about my weaknesses, so that the power of Christ can work through me. That's why I take pleasure in my weaknesses, and in the insults, hardships, persecutions, and troubles that I suffer for Christ. For when I am weak, then I am strong.

2 CORINTHIANS 12:8–10

In today's culture, it's common for people to brag about their achievements. They post their finest moments on social media and edit out all of their flaws. But not Paul. Paul brags only about his weakness. He knew the secret:

When we are inadequate, God gets all the glory. When we are weak, God is strong. When we aren't enough, we get *more* of God—more power, more miracles, more victory!

Dear All-Sufficient One,

I can't begin to comprehend Your power. Your resources are unlimited! I love that Your grace is sufficient for me. Father, I want to be weak because I want Your perfect power. You see my inadequacies, and You accept me just as I am. I give you my burdens and disabilities in exchange for Your confidence. Daddy, I believe You can even transform my weaknesses into strengths. I praise You in advance for doing the impossible, and I put all of my expectations in You.

When we believe the lie that we're inadequate, that's when Satan gets a foothold. It's almost like I take on that false identity and start agreeing with the less-powerful enemy. God is all-powerful. He is stronger than the lie of Satan. Why would I want to exchange His power for an inadequate power? God longs to come to our rescue. He longs to make us more than adequate. He prepares us and equips us. If we have faith and ask, anything is possible.

Omnipotent means having unlimited power, able to do anything. How does God being omnipotent change the possibilities for you?

The entire chapter of Hebrews 11 is dedicated to a list of people who were all inadequate but experienced God do the impossible through them. They all had two things in common—or make that three:

> How much more do I need to say? It would take too long to recount the stories of the faith of Gideon, Barak, Samson, Jephthah, David, Samuel, and all the prophets. **By faith** these people overthrew kingdoms, ruled with justice, and received what God had promised them. They shut the mouths of lions, quenched the flames of fire, and escaped death by the edge of the sword. **Their weakness was turned to strength.**

HEBREWS 11:32–34

So the first thing these heroes had in common: *They all had inadequacies.* Gideon was the least of his family and was frightened. Barak was a weak leader in battle. Samson made bad decisions, was blinded, and lost his physical strength. Jephthah made a stupid promise. David committed adultery and murder. Samuel almost wasn't even born!

The second thing they all had in common was that *they all had their weaknesses turned to strength*! Gideon became a mighty warrior. Barak led his army to victory. Samson became the strongest man alive and vanquished God's enemies. Jephthah led his people back to God. David became Israel's greatest king and was called "a man after God's own heart." Samuel heard God's voice when no one else could.

You'll have to read all of Hebrews 11 to discover the third thing they all have in common: *They all saw God's power perform miracles!*

Here's the truth in an equation: *Human **Inadequacy** + God's **Power** = A **Miracle** about to Happen.* We don't have to be strong; we just have to have faith. God's Word says that a tiny amount of faith is enough to move mountains (Matthew 17:20). You don't have to be stronger; you can ask God to give you more faith. You can exchange your weakness for God's omnipotence!

What are some areas where you feel weak?

Write a prayer asking God for His power, beginning with "Lord, empty me of all my fears, and fill me with Your strength."

When I feel insecure . . .
God is my BEST FRIEND

Did you ever go to extreme lengths to catch the attention or win the approval of someone else? My cousin once used duct tape to "wax" her eyebrows like the older girls at school—and lost half of her left eyebrow.

I used to sit on the beach with a giant book (upside down) when I was too young to read so I could be like my aunt who loved books. What was I thinking, missing all the fun in the water?

My brother once shaved his head into a ridiculous mohawk to look like the other boys on his baseball team.

Come on. I know you've done something . . . fess up!

Sometimes we think we have to look like someone else or act like someone else in order to be accepted. We might feel pressure to change who we are or to become something we aren't to get someone to like us. Have you ever noticed that when you are feeling insecure, all your fears and anxiety might be cured by one person choosing to accept you and be your friend or one boy giving you attention? While those friendships can be a gift, they can also leave a void because friends and boyfriends come and go.

God is my secure friend. He is always choosing me. Check out what Romans 5:8 says: "But God showed his great love for us by sending Christ to die for us while we were still sinners." We don't have to change who we were or change our behavior to receive God's approval. He loves us when we we're unlovable. Before we chose Him, He chose us!

This is what Jesus said to His followers: "I no longer call you slaves, because a master doesn't confide in his slaves. Now you are my friends, since I have told you everything the Father told me. You didn't choose me. I chose you" (John 15:15–16).

God didn't just choose me, He confided in me. That's what close friends do. When I moved to a new state in fourth grade, I had no friends. I quickly realized God was my Best Friend. Now I'm twenty-nine, and many of my friends are married and having babies. I'm still single, and even though God has blessed me with a few dear friends, He is still my Best Friend. God fills up the insecurities in my heart with His truth and love and His purpose for me. He gives me exactly what I need to make it through each moment of the day. He always shows up and never changes His mind about me. My other friends aren't my essential rock like Jesus is; they're just icing on the cake.

When I feel insecure, I feel lonely and different, like something is missing or wrong with me. What's wrong is that the focus is all on *me*! When I'm confident in my relationship with God, I'm not needy. People want to be around me because I'm speaking life and hope to others instead of worrying about myself: "But you are not like that, for you are a chosen people. . . . God's very own possession. As a result, you can show others the goodness of God, for he called you out of the darkness into his wonderful light" (1 Peter 2:9).

Dear Counselor,

We are all on the same path, searching for love and belonging. Thank You that my identity and purpose is in You alone. Instead of focusing on my own desire to be seen and heard, help me to smile and speak

*life to someone else who's struggling. I can share
Your hope with them. I can encourage them to
never give up. Wow, Lord, that changes everything.
My insecurity turns into purpose.*

Our identity turns that insecurity into purpose: "Once you had no identity as a people; now you are God's people. Once you received no mercy; now you have received God's mercy. Dear friends, I warn you as 'temporary residents and foreigners' to keep away from worldly desires that wage war against your very souls" (1 Peter 2:10–11).

Dear Trustworthy One,

*Thank You for seeing me in the darkness and not
keeping me there. Thank You for seeing my potential
and who I would become with Your strength.*

*Lord, help me not to fall into the trap of wanting
to be like the world because the acceptance the
world offers is unreliable. When I have a foot in
the world, I'm not completely sold out to You
and I'm avoiding what You want to do in and
through me. Help me to cherish my friendship
with You more than friendship with the world.
Thank You for being my lifelong companion.*

God wants us to be secure in Him. He designed us, so He delights in us far more than this world ever will. The trick is when you learn to make God your security, everything else falls into place. God will bring me friends and teach me how to be a friend when I find my security in Him alone and in being a part of His family.

Have you ever considered that maybe God is allowing you to experience feelings of insecurity or loneliness so you could see more clearly how much He loves you, so you would run back to Him instead of running to someone else to fill you up? Maybe you had forgotten whose you are!

Who are you? What three words best describe your true self.

1. _____

2. _____

3. _____

Along with these three describing words, you could add "child of God." If you have accepted Jesus as your Lord and Savior, you are a child of God! "See how very much our Father loves us, for he calls us his children, and that is what we are!" (1 John 3:1).

Dear Faithful Father,

To think that I was hand-picked and hand-chosen by You, oh Daddy, I can't stop smiling! To think before time existed You knew my name, You could hear my laughter, and You knew what color my eyes would be. Wow! You are my Creator and my Best Friend.

I want to fulfill the calling You have placed on my life. Help me not to shrink back. I want to experience more of You. Help me to shine with a hint of Your glory and shine with the hope that comes from You alone.

So, Daddy, I am reaching out my hand and touching Your garment to go on this journey with You because I know that is where the impossible becomes possible! That is where miracles happen. I put all my trust and focus on You!

Ask God to open your eyes to one person around you who could use a friend. Find a way to show that person how much he or she is loved by you and by your heavenly Father. Don't just think about it, go do it! Hurry, before that person goes to some extreme length, something they'll regret, just trying to fit in.

When I feel irritable . . .
God is UNCHANGEABLE

Do you ever feel like the only constant in life is change? Young women particularly can feel this way! Sometimes we learn to drive a car, graduate, change friend groups, move to a new city, and become responsible for our own bills all in the same decade. Combine any one of those major transitions with hormone and body changes, and you will probably have some moments where you just don't feel like yourself.

What are you most likely to do when you don't feel like yourself?

☐   Eat a gallon of ice cream

☐   Stay in bed all day

☐ Cry for no reason

☐ Binge on Netflix or rom-coms

☐ Scream and yell at the people you love most

☐ Other _____

Hormonal changes can make you say things you don't mean or cry all day for no reason! When you're struggling in a season of uncertainty or stressful change, you may unintentionally hurt friends and family members with your words. Your mood swings might make the people you love steer clear or walk on eggshells around you. There are always days (and sometimes especially that one week out of the month) when you just don't feel like yourself. Let's face it: one week a month equals one fourth of your life that you may feel more irritable. So, we need a plan to deal with it!

The good news is that no matter what changes you experience, whether big or small, your heavenly Father is unchanging. You can count on Him to stay the same when you can't count on anything else around you, including yourself. His Word makes some comforting claims about who He is and what we should do when we don't feel like ourselves. Consider what these verses say about who God is and about how God wants you to respond to Him.

"I am the LORD, and I do not change. . . .
Now return to me, and I will return to you,"
says the LORD of Heaven's Armies.

MALACHI 3:6–7

Who is God?

What does He want you to do?

Lord of Heaven's Armies,

Thank You that when everything else around me changes, You stay the same. I love knowing that when I don't feel like myself, I can run to You for truth and rest in Your strong arms. You are my safe haven and I am always secure in You. Thank You for coming close and listening to me. Thank You for your grace and mercy. Great is Your faithfulness.

Jesus Christ is the same yesterday, today, and forever. So do not be attracted by strange, new ideas. Your strength comes from God's grace.

HEBREWS 13:8–9

 Who is God?

What does He want you to do?

Dear Jesus, My Redeemer,

I know I'm going to make mistakes. That's why You came to die for me and make me new. Help me never to lose sight of who I belong to. Lord, I want to run to You because You are the same yesterday, today, and forever. Stop me when I start to run to something other than You to mask my pain or guilt. There is no shame near You, only grace. Remind me that Your grace is my greatest strength. Jesus, nothing compares to knowing You. My strength to go on comes from Your mercy and forgiveness, which is new every morning. I run to You this day! Comfort me with Your unchanging love.

Have you ever noticed that some people drain your energy when you spend time with them? A negative or a moody person isn't fun to be around. People either feel better or worse after spending time with you. You choose whether you speak life or death, whether you share positive thoughts or negative thoughts. My cousin Allie is such an encourager. After spending five minutes with her, I feel I can accomplish anything. She makes me feel good about myself. That's because she gets up every morning and spends time meeting with God, who is unchangeable. She says that it helps give her solid footing every day so she's prepared when surprises come her way. She doesn't get as flustered when she's had time to re-center her attitude and outlook each morning.

What if you made a conscious effort to speak life and speak positive encouraging words to every person you meet? Try pulling people up out of the pit instead of dragging them down with criticism. Smile and make eye contact with people at school or work. Be a friend to the friendless. Treat every person the way you want to be treated. When I'm feeling irritable, I'm usually focusing on myself instead of others. Turn your focus around. Open your eyes to the people who are hurting and need a boost all around you. It all begins by taking time daily to connect with your heavenly Father. Receive His gifts of love, joy, peace, patience, kindness, goodness, faithfulness, gentleness and self-control before tackling your day!

God calls you His "prized possession":

So don't be misled, my dear brothers and sisters. Whatever is good and perfect is a gift coming down to us from God our Father, who created all the lights in the heavens. He never changes or casts a shifting shadow. He chose to give birth to us by giving us his true word. And we, out of all creation, became his prized possession.

JAMES 1:16–18

 What does He want you to do? Write your own prayer to God based on truths you see in James 1:1.

When I feel jealous . . .
God is PERFECTION

 Name one quality, quirk, or talent that someone else has and deep down you wish you could have it too.

I have brown eyes. My brother has blue.

When we were little, he got a lot of attention for his blue eyes so naturally, I was a little bit jealous. I used to pray my brown eyes would miraculously turn blue. Then one day, I heard the story of a woman named Amy Carmichael who prayed the very same prayer. Every night, she asked God to change her eyes blue, and every morning, they were still brown. Later, she became a missionary to India and worked "undercover" pretending to be a local villager. God knew all along that if He had given her blue eyes, she wouldn't be able to fulfill her purpose because many people in India have brown eyes.

What are you jealous of? You are one of a kind. There is no one else like you. God is perfection. He designed you, and He doesn't make mistakes! King David said:

> "God's way is perfect.
>> All the LORD's promises prove true.
>> He is a shield for all who look to him for protection."
>
> 2 SAMUEL 22:31

David was the the youngest of eight brothers. When David's older brothers got to go fight important battles, he was left home taking care of the sheep. When God told the prophet Samuel to choose a king from among David's family, David's own father forgot about him and left him out of the lineup. As Samuel looked over each of the other taller, more-handsome brothers, God spoke to him and said, "Don't judge by his appearance or height. . . . The LORD doesn't see things the way you see them. People judge by outward appearance, but the LORD looks at the heart" (1 Samuel 16:7).

What does this sentence mean to you?
The LORD doesn't see things the way you see them.

How could that truth help you when you feel jealous? What might God be seeing that you don't see?

God sees the end from the beginning. He knows exactly what qualities and abilities you will need to fulfill His purpose for you. God didn't forget you when He gave talents to others. He chose to give you everything you have, and He also chose to withhold everything you don't have.

When we feel jealous of what someone else has, what we really have to decide is, Do we believe that God knows best? Do we believe that He is perfect?

Think about it this way: When you are jealous, who is your problem really with? It wasn't my brother's fault that he got blue eyes and I got brown. God decided what to give each of us. When I felt jealous, my problem wasn't really with my brother, my problem was with God. And guess what? I had eyes that worked! I could see. Someone who was blind would have loved to have my eyes. Now I have lots of vision deficits because of my brain injury and reading is very hard for me, but I am so grateful for what I do see.

One of life's greatest temptations is wanting what we don't have, or wanting what others have. That's jealousy.

> You want what you don't have, so you
> scheme and kill to get it. You are jealous
> of what others have, but you can't get it,

so you fight and wage war to take it away
from them. Yet you don't have what you
want because you don't ask God for it.
And even when you ask, you don't get it
because your motives are all wrong—you
want only what will give you pleasure.

JAMES 4:2–3

This verse implies that to fix your jealousy problem, you
have to fix your heart with God. God already knows that
you are jealous, so you might as well talk to Him about it.

 Identify one person you are jealous of and why.

Now try praying this prayer.

Lord Jesus,

Please give me a pure heart with pure motives,
a heart that desires what You desire and a heart
that seeks after You. I want to break free from
the grip of jealousy! I want to seek after You
and what matters in Your eyes because I believe
You see things I don't see. I believe Your way
is perfect. I trust that You know best.

I confess that I am jealous of

_____ .

Dear Lifelong Companion,

I only want to care about Your opinion,
Your motives, Your ways. I press into You today.
Father, please reveal to me my identity, who I am
in You. Thank You for giving me security.
Wow! What more could I be searching for?

Reveal the gifts and talents You have given me.
Help me understand how to use them for You and
for others. This life is not about me; it's about
making You famous. Help me not to use my gifts

and talents out of my own selfish motives; instead,
I want to use them to help people find You. I want to
bring honor and glory to Your Name. I don't
ever want to waste the gifts I have been given.

The next time you start feeling jealous try these simple steps.

1. *Tell God* (He already knows). Ask Him to fix your heart and your eyes.

2. *Praise God for what you* do *have.* Praise focuses on what I have been given, not on what I haven't been given. Make a gratitude list, praising God for your talents.

3. *Spend time developing your gifts.* When I'm using my gifts, it brings joy to my heart. When I'm trying to copy someone else's gifts, it exhausts and overwhelms me.

As you begin to fix your heart with God, you will find that His desires become your desires. Then you can ask Him for whatever you need or lack, and He will help you fulfill His purpose and dreams for you as He promises in His Word: "Take delight in the LORD, and he will give you your heart's desires" (Psalm 37:4).

All-Knowing Father,

Help me to delight in You. Lord, today I want to lay all of my desires at Your feet. Please fill me with Your desires and Your dreams. I don't want to limit You by my own fleshly wants. I am believing and asking for something greater!

Give me a new vision of who I am. I pray that I would embrace Your dreams. Your dreams make a difference for eternity. Your dreams outlast this life!

Give me a new vision of who I am!

When I feel less than . . . God is my CONTENTMENT

President Theodore Roosevelt once said, "Comparison is the thief of joy." And that was before Facebook and Instagram! It is almost impossible to be content with who we are or what we have when we are looking anywhere else but into the face of Jesus. Social media leaves me feeling *less than*. Looking at the girl next to me, who I think is prettier than I am, leaves me feeling *less than*. Pop culture leaves me feeling one step behind—always.

But when I look into the eyes of my Savior, I see that I am valuable. I am His beloved treasure: "For the LORD your God is living among you. He is a mighty Savior. He will take delight in you with gladness. With his love, he will calm all your fears. He will rejoice over you with joyful songs" (Zephaniah 3:17).

Dear Creator,

*You smile when You look at me. You delight in
me. No one else can fulfill the plan You have
prepared for me since the beginning of time.
Wow! Thank You that I am wanted by You.
I'm loving myself today because You chose me!
I can't even comprehend how You rejoice over me
with singing. Calm my fears about not being
enough and restore the joy that comparison
steals from me. You are my contentment!*

Comparison is another trap. Satan knows there will always be someone prettier, smarter, and more talented than I am. In my own strength, I will never measure up to others, but I have God Himself living inside of me. God wants me to break free from this comparison trap and to be comfortable in my own skin. God chose me before time existed. He could hear the sound of my laughter before I was born. God wants me to experience freedom from feeling less than He created me to be.

The slave does not have control or freedom to choose. God wants us to be free!

"So Christ has truly set us free. Now make sure that you stay free, and don't get tied up again in slavery to the law" (Galatians 5:1). Who or what is controlling you right now? How about your smartphone? Is it controlling you or are you controlling it? Snapchat? Instagram? If you must compare, track the minutes you spend on social media for a week and compare those minutes to the time you spend with the One who is your contentment. Maybe something else is enslaving your mind and time.

Is there anything you need to be set free from?

Dear Healer,

Today I am choosing to break free from the comparison trap. I am complete and secure in You. Help me see myself the way You see me—beautiful, confident, and hand-crafted by You. I am a child of the King! I don't want to be like anyone else. I want to stand out and be different and shine for You. Thank You that there is no one else like me. I praise You for I am fearfully and wonderfully made.

When I tap into God's power, I can move mountains. I can be anything He wants me to be. I can conquer the impossible. When I tap into God's power, I'm content to be me, content in my own skin, content in who I am in

Christ. God wants to fill us up with His confidence and security. He is the source that makes us more than we are. The apostle Paul understood this choice to be content:

> I know what it is to be in need, and I know what it is to have plenty. I have learned the secret of being content in any and every situation, whether well fed or hungry, whether living in plenty or in want. I can do all this through him who gives me strength.
>
> PHILIPPIANS 4:12–13 NIV

We can also find security and identity in the plans He has for us to fulfill on this earth. He gives us purpose and a reason to get out of bed each day. He has plans for us that only we can fulfill.

Try choosing contentment before comparing yourself. Say this out loud:

"I choose to be content that God knows best, content that God sees me, content that He will make a way no matter what my circumstances, content that I can trust Him while I am waiting for Him to act on my behalf, content that His will is bigger and greater than mine."

Merciful Father,

*My soul and heart can relax. You are my
contentment. I'm not worried about what is to come
because You hold my future. You hold the whole
world in Your righteous right hand. Nothing is
too hard for You. It's not even a challenge. I can
be content in Your embrace. Your peace washes
over me like a river. I can feel Your presence.
The less there is of me, the more there is of You!*

God delights in using people who are *less than*! The Bible is full of examples of ordinary people who accomplished extraordinary tasks so God would get all of the glory! Remember Moses, Gideon, David, and Peter?

John the Baptist said, "He must become greater and greater, and I must become less and less" (John 3:30). This forerunner and cousin of Jesus actually celebrated being "less than" so Jesus could fill the places where he was lacking and become more to the people around him. He chose to decrease so Jesus could increase.

The disciples were also content to deflect attention from themselves so that others would focus on Jesus: "When they saw the courage of Peter and John and realized that they were unschooled, ordinary men, they were astonished and they took note that these men had been with Jesus" (Acts 4:13 NIV).

According to Acts 4:13, who gets the glory when we are less than *others?*

In what ways could being less than *actually work to your advantage? Could being* less than *help Christ increase in you?*

List some ways that you feel less than: body image, intelligence, abilities, finances, etc.

Now try writing a prayer celebrating all of your less thans and asking Christ to fill those places and become greater in you!

When I feel like a failure . . . God is my PURPOSE

 WHO told you that you were a failure? Define failure in your own words.

WHEN did this lie get a foothold? Tell about it here.

Maybe you didn't make a singing group or sports team, didn't get a job you applied for, or didn't make good enough grades to get into the school you wanted. Maybe you don't have many friends, are trying to fit in, or are comparing yourself and think you can't measure up to the successful lives others "appear" to have on social media. Even highly successful people can still feel like a failure.

My dad always taught me to *fail forward*—that is, to learn from my mistakes and try something different. Failure is often the path to finding the purpose you were created to fulfill. Failure can create an opening for God to fill you with a new passion or vision.

A quick Google search will give you the definition of failure and its opposite, purpose! Failure is associated with lack of success, feeling like a loser, not performing well enough, and not feeling fulfilled. Purpose, on the other hand, is described as the reason for which something was created or exists.

Here is the great news: God gives you purpose. He even gives your failures purpose. When I feel like a failure, I am consumed with me and what others think of me. If God is my purpose, it takes the pressure off me. Instead I'm looking for hidden treasure each day. I'm looking for the plans God has for me and the divine appointments He will give me to speak truth and speak hope to others. Now that's fulfillment!

When you feel like a failure, try praying this prayer: "Lord, show me my purpose and calling today. What do You want to equip me for today?"

Right now claim this promise out loud: "I cry out to God Most High, to God who will fulfill his purpose for me" (Psalm 57:2).

God wants to use you to affect eternity—something way bigger than yourself! If you are fighting for something bigger than yourself, it keeps you going. Unwrap the gifts and passions God has given you. Discovering who you are in God's eyes helps you find your purpose in Him. When I started to see myself as God saw me, I didn't want to be known as the girl with the brain injury, I wanted to be known as the girl who loved Jesus and others with all of my heart. My purpose grew out of my identity in Christ.

 Ask God to give you a vision or dream for your life. Brainstorm here. Who do you want to impact? What can you do that will outlive you and last for eternity?

My Purpose = to give people hope and tell them God loves them; to be a friend to someone who is hurting worse than I am hurting.

Your Purpose =

Dear Daddy,

Please give me a big hug today, a tender touch from You. I am honored and grateful to be part of Your bigger plan. I know You don't need me, but the beauty is that You want to use me to accomplish the impossible for You. When I feel like a failure, You are my purpose and my confidence. Nothing else matters. Help take my eyes off of me and keep my focus on You. Thank You for creating me for a bigger purpose than myself. You are my motivation to get up in the morning. I can't wait to see the plans You have for me today.

Maybe you have messed up and you keep telling God I will never do (fill in the blank!) again. But you can't stop in your own strength, and so you feel like a failure. Addiction is a habit, a craving or dependency on something. Have you ever noticed that the more you do something the less you are satisfied? God wants to be your only addiction. The only "more" you need is Him. The more you spend time with Him and talk to Him, the more you will crave a relationship with Him. He is the only One who can satisfy the deepest longings of your heart and give you purpose that is greater than yourself.

Satan is your real enemy. He is a deceiver and a liar. He will tempt you to fill the void in your soul with any-thing but God to self-medicate your problems. The world will offer you lots of things to give you immediate and temporary pleasure. Over time those things become addictions and strongholds that control you. Once you fall into those temptations, Satan then turns around and accuses you. Revelation 12:10 says that Satan is "the one who accuses [you] before our God day and night."

Jesus isn't your accuser! He died on the cross to redeem you. He sits at the right hand of your Father in heaven interceding for you. He sent His Holy Spirit to live in you and help you discover the reason you were created. He fills your void with new purpose.

God is my PURPOSE

Lord Jesus,

I want my only craving to be my relationship with You. Protect my heart and mind. Break down any temptations that keep me from You. Thank You that I am loved and valued by You. The King of kings knows my name. Wow! Could I ask for anything more? Thank You that my past failures don't define me. My identity in You is not what the world thinks is important; it's far greater than I could ever imagine. You created me with eternity in mind.

Show me how I can break free of any addiction and run toward Your embrace. Today I receive Your grace and Your peace that passes all understanding.

I like the old saying "Today is the first day of the rest of your life." Keep moving forward with God's help. Don't let your past dictate who you are. God is your purpose, and He has things for you to accomplish for Him today that will impact eternity. He will repurpose your failures for His glory.

*Write your own prayer asking God to help you
break the chains of addiction and fill you with
His purpose instead.*

When I feel lonely . . . God is EVERYWHERE AT ALL TIMES

We can feel lonely for a lot of different reasons. Maybe you moved to a new town, just started a new school or a new job, and you think, *No one knows my name or even cares if I'm here.*

Perhaps a family member, who was supposed to protect you, hurt you. Maybe a trusted friend disappointed you, and now there is no one you can trust. Maybe a boyfriend just broke up with you.

Maybe you feel lonely in our society's current culture. You want to do what is right and honor God, but your friends are starting to make wrong choices. It is hard to stand alone and stand up for what is right.

Describe a time when you felt lonely.

Guess what? God knows your name. He has reserved a seat for you at the banquet table in heaven. He sent His Son, Jesus, to die on the cross so you could be there. You are never alone. God is always with you. No matter what happens on this earth, He is your lifelong companion. God is omnipresent, which means He is everywhere at once. God is before, behind, and all around you.

Psalm 139:2–5 helps us understand what *omnipresent* means:

> You know when I sit down or stand up.
> You know my thoughts even when I'm
> far away.

You see me when I travel
    and when I rest at home.
    You know everything I do.
You know what I am going to say
    even before I say it, LORD.
You go before me and follow me.
    You place your hand of blessing on
        my head.

God's omnipresence is hard for us to understand because
we are human, but God is not of our dimension. He isn't
earthbound. He is over the heavens and the earth. Nothing
goes unnoticed by God. He sees everything!

God is everywhere, plus His Spirit lives in our hearts. He
isn't only around us, He is in us. Wherever I go, He goes.
I'm a new person in Jesus:

> My old self has been crucified with Christ.
> It is no longer I who live, but Christ lives in
> me. So I live in this earthly body by trusting
> in the Son of God, who loved me and gave
> himself for me.
>
> GALATIANS 2:20

God's Spirit, who lives in me, is my source of strength and hope:

> But you belong to God, my dear children. You have already won a victory over those people, because the Spirit who lives in you is greater than the spirit who lives in the world.

1 JOHN 4:4

Dear Constant Companion,

It gives me so much comfort to know I'm never alone. Even when I feel lonely, You see me. You see my tears, my heartache. You see every injustice done to me. You see the battles I face. Because You are dwelling inside me, You understand me better than I understand myself. I can't hide from You because You are with me. Even in the darkness, You are there.

Sometimes God may take you through a season of loneliness because He has a purpose for you to fulfill that you wouldn't discover if you were surrounded by a lot of activity and friends. God planned to use Joseph to save people from starvation, but in order to get him where He wanted him, God first allowed Joseph to be put in a pit, then placed him as a servant in Potiphar's house; and later he was unfairly thrown into prison, seemingly abandoned. Those lonely situations came before God exalted Joseph into the palace to save the people of Egypt and surrounding nations from famine.

Joseph was sold by his own brothers into slavery, lived as a servant in a foreign culture, was accused of something he didn't do, and was forgotten by the people he helped. But the whole time he was alone, God's Word says over and over again that "God was with him." If Joseph had not gone through his lonely seasons, he would have missed his greatest purpose in life. Without that time alone with God, he would not have developed into the leader he became. After his seasons of growth and loneliness, God made him the second most influential man in the land!

Joseph eventually tells his brothers, "You intended to harm me, but God intended it all for good. He brought me to this position so I could save the lives of many people" (Genesis 50:20). God's purpose for Joseph was stronger than anything that others intended for him. God was with Joseph all the way!

Keep obeying God and doing what is right; He will honor you and lift you out of this lonely season. God has things for you to do. He has people for you to share God's love with.

Even if your earthly family is broken like Joseph's, you will always be a part of God's family. God's family is the church, and, believe me, God has so much for you to do. There are people all around you who are desperate to know God loves them.

Find a local church and use your gifts to serve others. God delights in using you in His kingdom work. He is looking for a heart that is available to Him. There is no greater fulfillment than when God is using you to help others. You won't feel lonely because you will be serving in God's family with a team of other people.

What skills has God given you? Brainstorm here.

Write a prayer asking God to help you use those skills to serve in a local church.

(Here are some ideas: hospitality team, social media team, worship team, prayer team, children's Sunday school teacher, greeter, feed and clothe the homeless, etc.)

Contact someone this week and let them know you are available to serve.

You are God's living, breathing ambassador. You are God's hands and feet on earth. God has things for you to do. You're God's mouthpiece for a time such as this. You can even give people hope with a smile. You are a reflection of Jesus. When you radiate the fruit of the Spirit to others, people will want to be around you. If you take a stand for Jesus, others will follow.

When I feel overwhelmed . . . God is my HELP & STRENGTH

Guess what? For the first time in thirteen years, I just typed these prayers you are about to read. I have never been able to see the "arrow" on the laptop screen before because my vision is severely impaired by my brain injury, but God is healing me beyond what is humanly possible! Woohoo! I might be exhausted after typing a couple of paragraphs, but I did it! The doctors said that after two years of therapy, I would be stuck and not see any more improvement in my brain. But I'm here to tell you that those doctors did not know who my Help and Strength was!

Father,

*You are good! Thank You for healing me
and helping me with Your unending strength.
No doctor can contain You. No diagnosis is too
difficult for You. You spoke the world into
existence. Nothing is too hard for You!*

Jesus,

*Thank You for whispering my name in Your
Father's ear and praying for me every day while
You sit at the right hand of our heavenly Daddy. You
are so kind and compassionate to remember that I
need You. You conquered death and the grave, yet
Your thoughts of me outnumber the grains
of sand. I am so overwhelmed by You!*

Holy Spirit,

*Keep it coming! I need more of Your power
and strength every moment of every day. I love that
You are named Helper. Who am I that the Spirit of
God would live inside of me and give me strength?
I can't comprehend You. You are impossible to
describe. All I can say is "holy, holy, holy" to You,
God Almighty, Three-in-One. Fill me up today.
Overwhelm me with ALL of You!*

Okay, now that we've had a praise party, write down the best thing about your life right now.

Next, what's the most overwhelming thing about your life right now?

God wants to be your Help and your Strength. You can be overwhelmed with Him or overwhelmed with the busy struggles of life. Think of your relationship with God as if He's knocking and ringing the doorbell, but you have to answer. He is waiting to spend time with us if we will just open the door and ask Him for help. Listen to Jesus describe how He wants to be with you: "Look! I stand at the door and knock. If you hear my voice and open the door, I will come in, and we will share a meal together as friends" (Revelation 3:20).

Jesus says that He wants to "share a meal together as friends." Can you get a mental picture of that? You are sitting down, taking a break from life, talking face to face, without your cellphone.

Do you know what the number-one relationship-blocker is today? You guessed it. It's our screens, especially our phones. Most humans admit to looking at their cellphones first thing in the morning. It's an addiction. We wake up to friend drama on group chats, behind on snapchat streaks, and comparing ourselves on social media. It's no wonder most mornings we feel overwhelmed before we even get out of bed!

Let's be honest: we're always on social media longer than we think and leave it feeling like we are less than what God thinks of us. Our screens leave our hearts and souls empty. We have a deep longing in our souls that only God can fill. So why do we open the door to social media before Jesus first thing in the morning?

Only Jesus knows what I am going to need to get through my day. He wants to fill me with greater gifts than anything my phone has for me. He offers me love, joy, peace, contentment, courage, help, and strength. Read these words out loud from Psalm 142:1–3:

I cry out to the LORD;
  I plead for the LORD's mercy.
I pour out my complaints before him
  and tell him all my troubles.
When I am overwhelmed,
  you alone know the way I should turn.
Wherever I go,
  my enemies have set traps for me.

Dear God,

It's Your girl. I come to You today with a heavy heart. A lot of things are on my mind. There are traps that the world is throwing my way, and I want to release them all into Your hands, for You are the firm foundation for my soul.

Daddy, please help me not to put any limitations on You. I want to come through these overwhelming

circumstances as an overcomer. I am not
defeated. I am more than a conqueror
because You will come to my rescue.

Continue reading and underline the phrase most meaningful to you:

I look for someone to come and help me,
   but no one gives me a passing thought!
No one will help me;
   no one cares a bit what happens to me.
Then I pray to you, O LORD.
   I say, "You are my place of refuge.
   You are all I really want in life."

PSALM 142:4–5

Jesus, my Best Friend,

I lift up my thoughts to You today. Please calm
my anxiety and fill me with Your thoughts that are
steadfast and true. I don't want to give Satan a
foothold or let him lead me astray. Help me bring
all of my overwhelmed feelings to You. Replace my
insecurities and doubts with the confidence of who
You are. You are my strength and my help. I run to
You today. You are all I want and all I need.

Who or what is your greatest enemy or time trap? Sit down and take a break face to face with Jesus for a minute. Eat some food while you are at it!

Did you know you can go into your settings on your cellphone and put limits on your own screen time? You can shut off your social media apps during certain hours of the day so you don't see it while you are trying to accomplish your most important goals for the day.

When I feel rejected . . . God is the LOVER OF MY SOUL

Have you ever felt rejected? Maybe your father, who was supposed to love and protect you, left you. Or maybe your friends didn't invite you to their party. Maybe a boyfriend broke up with you. Usually you can trace the feeling of rejection back to a specific event. It may have been something someone said or did intentionally or even unintentionally that hurt you and convinced you to start believing the lie that you are unwanted or unlovable.

Rejection becomes a foothold when we believe we aren't worthy of love. A foothold is any crack in the truth of who God is or how He sees you that causes you to open the door of your heart and mind to more lies from Satan, the enemy of your soul, or even lies from your own self.

You may start to feel like something is missing or wrong with you. If that happens, you need to pause and take time to immerse yourself in God's truth about who He is and whose you are.

 Take a moment to stop and pray and ask the Holy Spirit if there is a lie you have been believing about your identity. When have you felt rejected or unlovable?

Ask God to reveal how He sees you. Wait for a while in prayer, and then write down the words He brings to your mind or draw a picture of what you see in your mind.

Do you believe your heavenly Daddy loves you?
Pray and receive His unconditional love right now.

Psalm 62:1–5 describes how God is the Lover of my Soul. His love is the only thing that satisfies the deepest longings of my heart. Often we search for love in all the wrong places and forget that *God is love*! Read these words out loud:

> O God, you are my God; earnestly I seek you;
>   my soul thirsts for you;
> my flesh faints for you,
>   as in a dry and weary land where there is
>   no water.
> So I have looked upon you in the sanctuary,
>   beholding your power and glory.
> Because your steadfast love is better than
>   life,
>   my lips will praise you.
> So I will bless you as long as I live;
>   in your name I will lift up my hands.
>
> My soul will be satisfied as with fat and
>   rich food,
>   and my mouth will praise you with
>   joyful lips.

PSALM 63:1–5 ESV

Dear Lover of My Soul,

Thank You for smiling at me and delighting in me. Your love is so great I can't comprehend it. It was love that kept You on the cross. You paid the price so I could be priceless! Satan often lies to me, telling me I'm unworthy or that I've messed up way too much to be loved. Lord, I want to break free from that lie today.

Jesus, Your love transcends time and space. Nothing can touch it. Nothing is equal to it in power. Your love overcame everything on the cross. Your love is what keeps me going. It fills my heart with purpose, and I believe Your love fights for me. You modeled what true love is—how deep and great it is and how far it reaches. I want to press into Your everlasting love today.

Jesus met a woman who had felt rejected and unloved for twelve years. We don't even know this woman's name. She suffered from a bleeding illness, which according to Mosaic law (the rules in her culture), made her and anything she touched unclean. Can you imagine not being able to touch people or have them touch you? This woman wasn't even allowed to go into the temple to worship.

Then one day Jesus passed by. The woman had heard stories about how Jesus could heal people, so she pressed through the crowd to get near Jesus, just close enough to touch the hem of His garment, but not to be seen. We don't know if the woman felt unworthy to speak to Jesus or too unclean to ask permission to touch him after all of these years. All we know is that the moment she reached out to Jesus, she was physically healed. But not only her body was healed, her soul was healed too! Jesus didn't just love her enough to heal her illness, He loved her all the way to her core. She tried to stay hidden, but Jesus stopped to talk to her:

> A woman in the crowd had suffered for twelve years with constant bleeding, and she could find no cure. Coming up behind Jesus, she touched the fringe of his robe. Immediately, the bleeding stopped.
>
> "Who touched me?" Jesus asked. . . .
>
> . . . When the woman realized that she could not stay hidden, she began to tremble and fell to her knees in front of him. The whole crowd heard her explain why

she had touched him and that she had
been immediately healed.

"Daughter," he said to her, "your faith has
made you well. Go in peace."

LUKE 8:43–48

Jesus called this suffering woman something so personal
and intimate. He called her *daughter*. Because she had
faith in Jesus and reached out to Him, she was instantly
accepted. She became part of the family of God. Jesus
made her one of His own, the object of His affection.

Jesus saw beneath the woman's outward uncleanness. He
looked at her heart and honored her faith. He didn't see
an outcast; He saw a member of His family. He didn't
call her "rejected." He didn't even call her "woman"; He
called her "daughter." He gave her a forever family and a
home in heaven.

You were made exactly the way you are for God's glory.
Everything good or bad that has happened to you is being
repurposed to lead you closer to Jesus. All you have to do
is reach out and ask Him to make you at peace in your
body, mind, and soul. You can reach out to God through
prayer right now.

Try writing a prayer to God thanking Him for the privilege of being His daughter.

Ask the Holy Spirit to show you any places in your heart or mind where you need emotional healing. Write down what He reveals to you.

Pray this out loud and believe it:

Dear Heavenly Father,

Cradle me in Your everlasting arms today and show me how much You love me and delight in spending time with me. Lord, help me embrace Your love and never again believe the lie that I am rejected and unworthy of love. Thank You that Your love is so big and so strong that nothing I ever do or say can make it go away. I put all of my trust in You. In Jesus' name, Amen.

When I feel rushed . . .
God is ABLE

When I was in high school before the accident, I was a cheerleader and soccer player. School was hard for me so I had to study extra hours to make good grades. I didn't have any time to spare. I knew I needed God's help, and I wanted to make Him my top priority; so I started setting my alarm a half hour early to sit in my lime green chair and spend time with Him. That is when I started journaling my prayers to God and reading the New Testament for the first time on my own. I didn't just read it, I used colored pens and highlighters and talked to God about what I was reading. I asked Him to help me understand His words and apply them to my life. The more I did it, the more I craved it! God would meet me in that chair. It felt like He was tangibly there giving me a big "hug" for the day. He would whisper encouragement to my heart through His written words. Every morning He gave the exact courage and strength I needed to conquer the day. He gave me His perspective on what was important. That's how I first began to totally rely on Him.

When and where do you like to spend time with God? Sketch a drawing of your favorite place to meet with God:

You can meet with God anywhere and anytime. It doesn't have to be in the morning, but I have found that meeting with God first before I do anything else does have a few benefits:

- If I meet with God first, I don't run out of time for Him.

- When I meet with God first, I seem to be able to accomplish more.

Time with God calms my heart, clears my mind, and miraculously makes a way for me to accomplish more than I could if I attacked the day on my own. I need Him to act on my behalf, so I've found that I don't have time *not* to meet with Him.

The psalmist explains this beautifully: "I rise early, before the sun is up; I cry out for help and put my hope in your words" (Psalm 119:147).

 Can you think of other benefits to meeting with God first before your day begins?

When I try to do things in my own strength, I get overwhelmed. When I press into God for more of His strength, He seems to stretch time. I am able to do far more with Him than without Him because He is able to do the impossible.

God's Word tells us the winds and the waves know Jesus' name; I bet time does too! God can even slow down time. He did that for Joshua during one of his battles. God made the sun stand still so the Israelites could win:

> On the day the LORD gave the Amorites over to Israel, Joshua said to the LORD in the presence of Israel:
>
>> "Sun, stand still over Gibeon,
>>> and you, moon, over the Valley of Aijalon."
>
>> So the sun stood still,
>>> and the moon stopped,
>>>> till the nation avenged itself on its enemies,
>
> as it is written in the Book of Jashar.
>
> The sun stopped in the middle of the sky and delayed going down about a full day.

There has never been a day like it before or since, a day when the LORD listened to a human being. Surely the LORD was fighting for Israel!

JOSHUA 10:12–14 NIV

Dear Miraculous One,

Sometimes I feel like I'm running out of time or that I don't have enough time. Lord, I want to lift those thoughts to You. I want to break free from that trap! Time here on this earth is short, but I want to praise You, the Author of time, that I can rest in You this day.

Lord Jesus, thank You that You can slow down time. I love how You literally stopped time for Joshua and how You are still able to stretch time for me this day. Lord, You are the same yesterday, today, and forever, so I just want to praise You for being sovereign over the time factor in my life. Help me take hold of my moments and my time and not waste any of them, because I want to bring honor and glory to You in all the time I am given here on this earth.

*So Good Shepherd, lead, guide, and direct me
every single step of the way and direct my time
so I can use it best to bring honor and glory to
Your perfect name—Jesus, Jesus, Jesus.*

Just repeating the name of Jesus over and over out loud when I'm in a rush helps me refocus my brain from feeling panicked about time to having peace that God is able to make everything work out. Besides, God's time frame is far different than ours. He thinks about eternity when we think about our to-do lists. Sometimes He chooses to interrupt our to-do lists with something far more important. When He does, you can trust that He is able to accomplish everything that concerns you. Often He will even accomplish more!

Write your own prayer to God based on this claim about God in Ephesians 3:20:

"Now all glory to God, who is able, through his mighty power at work within us, to accomplish infinitely more than we might ask or think."

My grandpa, Dr. Ed Hindson, always says, "If you can trust God for eternity, you can trust Him for today." Make a list of everything you need to accomplish today. Then pray the prayer you just wrote over this list. Ask God to accomplish everything you need or something greater!

Today's To-Do List:

1. _____

2. _____

3. _____

4. _____

5. _____

6. _____

When I feel shame . . .
God is my
RIGHTEOUSNESS

You don't usually go around telling people that you feel ashamed. Shame is a hidden feeling or heaviness you carry deep in your heart. It's different from guilt. Guilt is feeling bad about a poor choice you made. Shame is feeling bad about *who* you are. You resent yourself, blame yourself, despise yourself.

If you carry shame, you are believing a lie about your identity. Maybe you believe you are unworthy of love. When that happens, you start to hate yourself instead of hating your sin. You take on the identity of your sin. You believe things like *I'm a liar, I'm a thief, I'm an addict* instead of believing the truth: *I am priceless, I am made right through Christ, I am a child of God!*

Shame is never from God. It's got Satan's fingerprints all over it. When God convicts us of sin in our lives, it's never to condemn us, but to free us, cleanse us, and make us whole again. We know this because of what God promises us in His Word: "Those who look to him [God] for help will be radiant with joy; no shadow of shame will darken their faces" (Psalm 34:5).

Heavenly Father,

Expose the shame in me for what it is, a lie about my identity. When I feel shame, I can't get past myself. That's not who I am. I am a new creation in You. Overwhelm me with Your radiant joy! Forgive my sins and take every shadow of shame away from my heart. I pray that not even a trace of it could be found on my face. I want people to see only You when they look at me.

Daddy, You promise that if I seek You, I will find You. Give me more of Your character. Transform me. Trade my mess for Your righteousness. Be my personal craftsman. Mold me and shape me into a beautiful vessel that reflects Your character. Become my whole identity!

Shame stems all the way back to the garden of Eden. When Adam and Eve disobeyed God and ate of the Tree of the Knowledge of Good and Evil, they felt shame for the first time and hid from God. Shame is not from God because it separates us from Him. God wants to be near us; that's why He came walking in the garden, looking for Adam and Eve.

The serpent, which was the devil himself, twisted the truth to trick Eve. He knew if she and Adam ate the fruit, they would become aware of good and evil. Before that time, Adam and Eve "were both naked, but they felt no shame" (Genesis 2:25). God never intended for us to feel shame, but Satan couldn't wait for us to experience it because He knew it would make us want to run from God. Satan uses similar tactics today. He entices us to sin and then he turns around and accuses us before God (Revelation 12:10).

God does just the opposite. The very first thing God did for Adam and Eve, while they were still blaming each other for their sin, was to provide a remedy for their shame. In the middle of explaining the consequences of their sin, God does something remarkable that tells us something very important about who He is: "At that moment their eyes were opened, and they suddenly felt shame at their nakedness. So they sewed fig leaves together to cover themselves. . . . And the LORD God made clothing from animal skins for Adam and his wife" (Genesis 3:7, 21).

Can you imagine being naked and trying to cover yourself in leaves? But guess what? God didn't wait to come to their rescue. He didn't watch them struggle. He provided a covering from animal skins that would last a lot longer than fig leaves. In doing so, He demonstrated that He longs to take away our sin and provide a way for us to be made right in His eyes.

God made animal-skin coverings to demonstrate that one day He would offer a permanent covering for our sin. He would exchange our wrongdoing (the things that cause you shame) for His righteousness. He planned before the creation of the world to send Jesus to die on the cross as a permanent sacrifice to pay for our sins past, present, and future. But He didn't just take on our sins, He offered us His identity, the essence of who He is, in exchange for our sins: "God made him who had no sin to be sin for us, so that in him we might become the righteousness of God" (2 Corinthians 5:21 NIV).

Do you want to take on God's identity? He gives you His righteousness in exchange for your sin. When you repent and ask Him to be your Savior and forgive your sins, He no longer sees any of the wrong things you have done. He sees you as a new creation. You become just as if you have never sinned. You become God's righteousness! Wow! That isn't just a moment-changer, that's a life-changer!

Would you like to exchange the lies you are believing about your identity for the truth? Take a few minutes to pray through these questions. You may want to ask a friend or mentor you trust to pray through them with you and help agree with what the Holy Spirit reveals to you. God promises, "Where two or three gather together as my followers, I am there among them" (Matthew 18:20). He wants to come and remove your hidden shame today!

Take a moment and ask God, "When did I start wearing the label of shame? Was there an event or something someone said to me?" Ask God to reveal to you the root *of where the shame came from.*

Ask God to show you how He sees you. What does God want to give you in place of shame?

When I feel trapped . . .
God is WITH ME
until He delivers me

The night my family got hit by a drunk driver, my dad almost lost his life because he was trapped. Our van was so warped that our county rescue volunteers could not get him out of the twisted metal shell, and he was losing blood fast. He needed a miracle, which came in the form of an off-duty fireman who happened to see the accident and came to his rescue. No one had been able to get to my dad, but this experienced, city-trained fireman knew how to get an IV into my dad's arm before he was finally cut free from the wreckage. That IV saved his life!

The real miracle for my dad that night wasn't his deliverance. That was coming. The real miracle was the IV that extended his life while he was waiting to be free.

The same is true for you and me when we feel trapped. Deliverance is coming one day for us, but we may need God to deliver hope, joy, protection, or wisdom while we are waiting to break free.

Are you feeling trapped in any of these ways?
(Circle the words that relate to you.)

Broken family   Unhealthy relationship

Weight   Job or no job

Financial stress   Wrong friend group

Doubts   Schoolwork

Mental illness   Physical illness/Disability

Abuse   Addiction

Other _____

Maybe you feel trapped in your mind. Maybe you thought your life would turn out differently. When I used to dream about my future, I thought by now I'd be married, or have a certain job, or have kids. I'm still waiting for God to heal me, but while I'm waiting, I don't want to miss the miracle of God being *with* me.

One of my favorite Old Testament stories is the parting of the Red Sea. Before God parts the waters, there's a big life-changing aspect of the story that usually gets over-looked. Let's read it and see if you can find it.

> Then the angel of God, who had been leading the people of Israel, moved to the rear of the camp. The pillar of cloud also moved from the front and stood behind them. The cloud settled between the Egyptian and Israelite camps. As darkness fell, the cloud turned to fire, lighting up the night. But the Egyptians and Israelites did not approach each other all night.
>
> Then Moses raised his hand over the sea, and the LORD opened up a path through the water with a strong east wind. The wind blew all that night, turning the seabed into dry land. So the people of Israel walked through the middle of the sea on dry ground, with walls of water on each side!
>
> EXODUS 14:19-22

Everybody talks about the parting of the Red Sea, but most everyone misses the movement of God, the cloud and fire that protected the Israelites from the Egyptians while they were waiting to be delivered. Before God rescued them by parting the water, He was already there, already with them, surrounding and protecting them on all sides.

Sweet friend, don't miss the miracle in the waiting! You may be angry or confused because God hasn't rescued you yet. You may not understand why you are still trapped in your family or addiction or illness. But I can promise you this: you are never alone. God is with you until He delivers you.

Dear Almighty Deliverer,

I want to rest in You as I'm waiting. Thank You for showing me Your majesty through this trial and giving me more of Your presence. I get to see You do things You have never done before because I am trapped with my brain injury. So I praise You for being trapped, even trapped in my mind. Fill me with Your hope and joy while I wait for Your strong deliverance. I trust in You alone this day, my Defender, my Comfort, my close Companion.

Being trapped by the Red Sea gave the children of Israel the opportunity to see God do the impossible. He created a pathway no one knew was there! And word of God's power spread all over the known world. Ultimately, being trapped wasn't a curse; it was a blessing!

One of the ways being trapped in my brain injury has benefited me is that it's changed my dreams! I no longer think just about getting married, or having a job or kids, I dream about using my injury to change the world! God trapped me in my disability so I'd have more of His ability!

> But forget all that—
>> it is nothing compared to what I am
>>> going to do.
> For I am about to do something new.
>> See, I have already begun! Do you not
>>> see it?
> I will make a pathway through the
>> wilderness.
>> I will create rivers in the dry wasteland.

ISAIAH 43:18–19

Dear Comforter,

I praise You! I want to rest in Your goodness, grace, and mercy. Thank you, Daddy, that You see me and see the hardship I am going through. Thank You for carrying me. I need You; I need You so much. I am choosing today to trust in You with all my heart and to believe in miracles because You are the

*God of miracles. Lord Jesus, I don't know
what the end result will be, but I can put my hope
in Your name because You are in it with me!*

*In regard to my future, I trust it to You. You
are above the heavens and the earth, above my
imagination. When I hold on to Your hand, anything
is possible. Fill me with new dreams and new
desires. I want to walk on water with You.
I trust my future to You.*

God has new dreams, new thoughts, and new experiences for you. Sometimes the only way to experience these new things is to forget the old things. Quit *mourning* what you've missed and *celebrate* the new thing God is doing. God is good! He has your best interest in mind! Try shifting your focus from feeling trapped to expecting the new thing He is about to do.

 Can you think of anything good that has come out of you feeling trapped?

Try writing your own prayer thanking God for being with you until He delivers you:

When I feel treated unfairly . . . God is my DEFENDER

When was the last time you were overlooked, wrongly accused, discriminated against, or treated unfairly in some way? If you have siblings or roommates, I'm sure there have been times you were blamed for things that were not your fault. Part of growing up involves learning how to respond to injustice in a positive, healthy way.

Often, our go-to response is to get angry because we want the unfair wrong to be made right. Left alone, anger usually leads to isolation or retaliation. If you have been hurt in the past, you're tempted to put up walls to protect yourself, walls to keep you safe. Maybe you made a vow that "no one will ever hurt me again or treat me unfairly again" so you don't let anyone get close to you.

Satan loves to get us to feel alone. He tempts us with the lie that no one can be trusted and no one understands. The truth is that Jesus was treated unfairly and tempted just like you. God knows exactly how you feel, and He longs to defend you. His Word promises: "The LORD is your mighty **defender,** perfect and just in all his ways; Your God is faithful and true; he does what is right and fair" (Deuteronomy 32:4 GNT).

Do you believe God can protect and defend you? Try writing a prayer in your own words asking Jesus to defend you:

God is my DEFENDER

Jesus, Jesus, Jesus,

*Thank You for Your mercy that is new every day.
Thank You for being my Defender. It's not just a
dream or a far-off wish; it's true! I stand on the
solid truth that You will fight for me and protect me.
Lord, I put my security in You because You came to
live on earth so You would understand everything
I feel! Help me move forward in confidence today.
Equip me, heal me, and defend me!*

Sometimes we choose to stay angry because it makes us feel like we're in control. When I'm not trusting God to defend me, I have an all-consuming desire to protect myself. My anger becomes a control issue. I'm fighting to be in control of every situation so I don't get mistreated again. God never asked me to protect myself. I have to stand on the truth that God will defend me when I "let go" and put my unfair situation in His hands. I have to trust that God can defend me better than I can defend myself.

Do you believe God can defend you better than you can defend yourself? Are you acting like you believe this?

Take a moment to ask God, "Lord, where am I not allowing You to fight for me?"

If you are scheming ways to get even or having imaginary conversations in your head with the person who wronged you, chances are you are not fully trusting God to defend you. Retaliation may feel good for a moment, but it does not compare to experiencing God's blessings that come from trusting Him.

 If you are struggling to "let go and trust God," write down this verse where you will see it every day: "Don't repay evil for evil. Don't retaliate with insults when people insult you. Instead, pay them back with a blessing. That is what God has called you to do, and he will grant you his blessing" (1 Peter 3:9).

One of the best real-life examples from the Bible of trusting God instead of repaying evil was David, the teenage kid who defeated the giant Goliath. He won a huge battle for King Saul so you'd think Saul would have loved him, right? Nope! King Saul later became jealous of David and tried to kill him. David had to run and hide in caves. One time, Saul entered a cave to use it as a bathroom—and it happened to be the very cave where David was hiding! It was the perfect opportunity for David to get even. He could easily have killed Saul. But David believed revenge and justice were God's job, not his, so he spared Saul's life and trusted God to defend him. Saul ended up dying in battle, and God elevated David to be one of Israel's greatest kings! Here's what David said:

> "The LORD rewards everyone for their righteousness and faithfulness. The LORD delivered you [Saul] into my hands today, but I would not lay a hand on the LORD's anointed. As surely as I valued your life today, so may the LORD value my life and deliver me from all trouble."
>
> 1 SAMUEL 26:23–24 NIV

When someone treats me unkind or unfairly, I try to remind myself that hurting people hurt others. It helps me to see past their actions and realize that they are more wounded than I am. They have insecurities they are trying to cover up. Look at King Saul. He was insecure because the people in his kingdom praised and valued David more than they valued him. In the end, Saul ended up being miserable and David ended up being king. If David had tried to defend himself, he could have destroyed his life like Saul. Anytime we try to do God's job, it doesn't end well. God's job is to defend us. Our job is to trust Him.

Dear Protector,

I want to break free from the chains of feeling like I have been treated unfairly. Those negative consuming thoughts take my focus away from true thoughts about You! Father, protect me today with the truth of who You are. I trust You to defend me. I open my grip of control and release the situation into Your hands. Just saying those words helps me breathe a sigh of relief and REST in Your arms.

Thank You that I am victorious in Your eyes. Help me to bless those who want to hurt me. I know that I can trust You to lift me up.

Write a prayer, asking the Holy Spirit to reveal if you are trying to defend yourself to anyone.

Is there a situation that God wants you to stop trying to control and give over to Him so He can defend you?

Ask God to help you receive His peace and protection. He wants to give it to you.

When I feel uncertain . . . God is TRUTH

Life is kind of like a book. Do you ever wish you could just skip ahead a few chapters and see how your life is going to turn out? There are so many questions I have about my future, like will I ever get to drive, will my memory improve, who will I marry, will I ever have children? Sometimes I wish I could sneak a peek at the last chapter to see what happens! Then I think, *Spoiler alert!* If I knew the future, I would miss the priceless moments of walking with God, communicating back and forth, learning to hear His voice, waiting on Him, and discovering His amazing confirmations. I would never want to miss those treasures!

What's your favorite fiction book or series of all time?

Did you ever skip ahead to read the end of the book or did you read every page in order?

What movie or streaming series are you most looking forward to being released in the next twelve months?

Will you read any spoilers or watch the last episode before you've watched all the others?

There's a reason they call the people who tell what happens at the end of a movie or book "spoilers"—they ruin the experience! When we don't know what's going to happen, we stay fully engaged with the storytelling, hanging on all the twists and turns of the movie's or book's plot. The same is true when we're trusting God with the future.

Because we don't know what's going to happen, we hope more, pray longer, try harder, and believe bigger.

Remember the first time you tried out for a role on a team or a new job? You probably could not wait for the announcement of the outcome. I used to be a cheerleader. After every tryout, the coach would call each participant to let us know if we made the team. I remember sitting by the phone all night, waiting for that phone call. That phone had my full attention and devotion.

That's why God allows us to feel uncertain at times. He longs to be the focus of our attention and hopes. He longs to fill us with His plans. That happens best when we aren't sure what to do. When we feel uncertain, He is our truth. Uncertainty was never meant to lead us to bondage or anxiety or fear, but to bring us closer to Jesus and ultimately to His peace and freedom. Knowing the truth is meant to set us free.

"Then you will know the truth, and the truth will set you free" (John 8:32). What two promises can you claim from this verse?

1. _____

2. _____

First, God promises that you *will know*. Be comforted with this thought: God wants you to know the truth even more than you want to know it! He will reveal His truth in His time.

Think about this: Everything you are feeling uncertain or worried about is already accomplished in heaven. It's already been DONE! Every decision you are stressing over is finished in His hands. Stay close to Him, and He will guide you into His truth that already exists, past-tense in heaven. He already wrote the end of your story!

Second, God promises His truth will *set you free*. It doesn't mean God's plan is going to be easy, but it means He will make a way through the wastelands, He will carry you with peace through the fire, He will use you to be a light in the darkness, He will strengthen your spirit and fill your mind with certainty. When we put our hope in Him, anything is possible. We break free from our earthly reality and experience miracles of His heavenly kingdom in this life, which are magnified in our moments of uncertainty.

God of Truth,

So much about my future is up in the air. I love that You are my secure truth and I can rest in Your everlasting arms. I know the truth sets us free, and

*freedom is found in You. It doesn't mean I will
know all of the answers today, but I can trust
that You have my best interest in mind.*

*You are my Good Shepherd, and You will lead,
guide, and direct me one step at a time. I don't have
to know what tomorrow will bring because I can
trust You for today. You want me to be desperate
for You, to cling to You and go where You lead.
In the place of uncertainty, You will equip me to do
the impossible. The best place I can be is in Your
arms, just resting! You are my certainty!*

Here are a handful of solid concepts to lean on when you
are feeling uncertain:

First, *Truth is a Person*: "Jesus told him, 'I am the way,
the truth, and the life. No one can come to the Father
except through me'" (John 14:6). Truth is not just
knowledge or information. Truth isn't one decision or
another. Truth is a Person! When you aren't sure what
to do, move closer to the One who is Truth (Jesus) and
stick near Him. Finding certainty is less about which
path you take and more about being near the Person
who planned your path.

Next, *truth never changes*: "Jesus Christ is the same yesterday, today, and forever" (Hebrews 13:8). Today's culture

sways back and forth like the wind based on public opinion and what feels good. It puts pressure on us to change with it, making it difficult at times to discern the right voices. Culture idolizes the individual's rights, making it attractive to fall prey to its whims. Circumstances also change, sometimes weakening my resolve to stand firm.

Sweet friend, don't give up. Hold on to Jesus. Circumstances may change and culture may change, but truth never changes. Truth is absolute. It is the same yesterday, today, and forever. It's a rock you can always count on because the Person of Truth (Jesus) never changes.

Third, *it's easy to access truth*: "Make them holy by your truth; teach them your word, which is truth" (John 17:17). God's Word is truth. Scripture is our guidebook. It's our security. It's never empty or wasted. Quoting Scripture out loud can penetrate our hearts and cement the truth in our minds. We believe what we say out loud. God's Word will deliver us, redeem us, fill us with new passions, and overwhelm us with unfailing love. When you need to know the truth, run to God and His Word. It's as easy as opening the Bible app on your phone! Read until God shows you something that feels like He wrote it just for you!

Daddy,

When I feel uncertain, my peace is anchored in You. You are the one thing that stays the same and never changes. You are Truth. Your Word is truth. Your Word is alive and powerful and can penetrate every part of my soul that is questioning and looking for purpose and meaning. You see my circumstances, and You are in authority over every challenge and decision I am facing. When I don't know which way to turn, I listen for Your voice saying, "This is the way to go."

Lord, I run to You with my dreams, my hopes, my desires, and my insecurities. Help me hear Your voice louder than any other voice. Today I claim that You are Truth for me!

What is your greatest uncertainty right now? Write it down on a separate sheet of paper. Then turn the paper over and write down this truth from God's Word:

"When the Spirit of truth comes, he will guide you into all truth. . . . He will tell you about the future."

JOHN 16:13

When I feel wounded . . .
God is my HEALER

A drunk driver changed my life forever. He took a lot of things from me. He took my teenage years from me. He gave me a brain injury, which causes me pain and suffering every day.

You may not have physical wounds, but we all have emotional wounds. Maybe a friend betrayed you, maybe a parent abandoned you, maybe someone you trusted lied to you. Emotional wounds can be the most painful of all, and many times they are hidden away deep within our hearts. I want you to know that God sees deep down inside your heart. He weeps over what hurts you, and He wants to heal your wounds. His Word says that, "He heals the brokenhearted and bandages their wounds" (Psalm 147:3).

Dear Almighty Healer,

*In my darkest moments, You are always there
to cradle me in Your arms. I trust my wounded heart
to You. I don't want to hold on to the emotional pain
any longer. Please heal me from the inside out.
You can bring beauty from ashes. You can mend
my broken heart one stitch at a time. Thank you for
healing my heart and my thoughts beyond what is
humanly possible. I put all of my trust in You!*

Jesus was wounded too. The things He said while He was on the cross help us understand who God is and how to begin the healing process when we are hurting. According to Jesus' example, the first step to healing is forgiveness. If you have been wounded by someone, you know forgiveness is really hard. Because of the pain involved with our wounds, forgiveness is often misunderstood.

Test your own understanding by answering True or False:

A person should not be forgiven until he/she is sorry for their actions.
☐ TRUE ☐ FALSE

You cannot feel angry or hurt and genuinely forgive.
☐ TRUE ☐ FALSE

You have not really forgiven until you have forgotten.
☐ TRUE ☐ FALSE

Genuine forgiveness takes time.

☐ TRUE ☐ FALSE

I have the ability to choose forgiveness.

☐ TRUE ☐ FALSE

It might surprise you that the answer to every single statement according to Jesus' example is *False*. Surprised? One of the best ways to understand what forgiveness *is* may be to understand what forgiveness *is not*. Let's look at how Jesus handled forgiveness when he was most wounded: "When they came to a place called The Skull, they nailed him to the cross. And the criminals were also crucified—one on his right and one on his left. Jesus said, 'Father, forgive them, for they don't know what they are doing'" (Luke 23:33–34).

Forgiveness is not conditional. No one was saying that they were sorry when Jesus shouted forgiveness from the cross. Forgiveness is unconditional. It has nothing to do with your offender or the offense, but it has everything to do with your healing and your heart. If you are waiting for the people who have wounded you to say they are sorry, you aren't really forgiving; you're taking a gamble. Do you really want to gamble with your heart and your potential to heal? Your offenders may not ever ask for your forgiveness. They may not even realize how much they've hurt you or be around to make it right. You may have done nothing to deserve your pain, but you can move beyond it with the God's help.

Forgiveness is not feeling good about something bad that happened. After Jesus extends forgiveness, He still shouts out in pain, "My God, my God, why have you forsaken me?" (Matthew 27:46 NIV). Your heavenly Father does not minimize your pain. He sent His Son to the cross to feel your pain. Similarly, you don't have to endorse the injustice of abuse, neglect, injury, theft, or whatever sin you are the victim of to initiate forgiveness. Anger and pain are God-given emotions meant to identify the fact that something is wrong and action needs to be taken. Your heavenly Father does not frown upon your anger. He too feels angry over injustice. Forgiveness does not require the absence of pain or anger because forgiveness is not a feeling; it's an action.

Forgiveness is not forgetting. Jesus never forgot the cross, yet He forgave the ones who put Him there. He used the cross to turn what was meant for evil into something good. There is one big flaw with the theory "Forgive and forget"—it's not humanly possible. God wired our brains to hold on to things that hurt. In that sense, God wired us to need His help and forgiveness every day. You may never forget, but you can be healed when you forgive.

Forgiveness does not have to take a long time. The first statement Jesus said out loud on the cross was "Father, forgive them." While they were still driving the nails in His hands, He was forgiving them! It seems as though Jesus was teaching us that it's easier to forgive the sooner we forgive. I'm not shaming you if it is taking you a long time to forgive. We may think we are too hurt to forgive, but what if we are hurting ourselves more by delaying forgiveness? Jesus modeled that we can begin forgiving as soon as we are wounded, before the bitterness has time to take root.

Forgiveness is not possible in our own strength. Notice that Jesus prays and asks His Father for help. He never summons the words, "I forgive you." He prays, "Father, forgive them." He forgives His offender by asking His Father to do it for Him. We can do the very same thing when forgiveness seems impossible. Try saying the words of Jesus, "Father, forgive them," when it hurts too much to forgive.

The reason I wanted to forgive was because I wanted to be free. I like to call forgiveness "FREE-giveness." I didn't want anything or anyone to consume my thoughts but Jesus. Before I chose forgiveness, the drunk driver had power over me. I was giving Satan permission to hurt me emotionally again and again. Bitterness was like a toxin spreading through my body. After I forgave, I felt free to use my story to make a difference in the world.

One thing that helps me forgive is to visualize taking the drunk driver "off of my hook" and putting him on "God's hook." I no longer expect him to pay for what he did to me. I have given him to God. He's on God's hook. Jesus paid for what he did to me when He died on the cross, so why would I hold against him what Jesus already covered?

Besides, I had to remember all the times that God had forgiven me and given me grace. Knowing that I was forgiven helped me make the choice to forgive. Colossians 3:13 says: "Bear with each other and forgive one another if any of you has a grievance against someone. Forgive as the Lord forgave you" (NIV).

Another thing that helped me was praying daily for the drunk driver. Bitterness cannot grow while you are praying for someone. I wanted to stay free of bitterness, so I started to pray for my offender and asked Jesus to help me forgive him. In my situation, my offender was not physically able to say he was sorry or fix what he had done to me. He is still more injured than I am, so I decided to write him a letter and let him off of my hook.

I still have never talked to him, but I am free. Forgiveness does not mean everything gets fixed perfectly. Forgiveness means you are free to receive all the love and hope God has for you. One day everything will get fixed perfectly in heaven, where there is no more sorrow or pain. Until then, we have forgiveness.

Dear Drunk Driver,

My name is Jennifer Barrick, I don't know if you know who I am, but I am a young woman who prays for you every day. I am asking God to heal you so that you can talk and walk again! One day I hope to pray over you in person, but more importantly, I want to meet you in heaven one day—where there is no more pain and no more tears.

I have a brain injury because you were drinking and driving and I have suffered a lot too. I like to think that God "remolded me" and made me "better." Even though I have disabilities and struggle every day, God is using me in ways I never dreamed possible for His Glory.

I want you to know that I have FORGIVEN you—not in my own strength but in God's strength. I can't explain it, but God has given me a special love for you. I will continue to pray for you daily.

Today, Lord, I choose to forgive just like you forgave me. Thank you for second chances.

Love, Jen

Let God start healing your broken heart right now. Write your own letter of forgiveness to whoever wounded you. You can give the letter to them or just give it to God. If you still can't forgive, just write, "Father, forgive

_____."

When I feel unlovable . . . God is LOVE

Every girl I have ever met was created with a special longing to be loved. That's why we flock to rom-coms, daydream about our wedding day, and imagine being picked out of a crowd of thousands by some worthy Prince Charming who will cherish us just as we are—without makeup, pretending, or pressure to perform or achieve. God reveals this mystery concerning women when He commands husbands to "love your wives, just as Christ loved the church" (Ephesians 5:25). He had other commands for how women should love their husbands, but the Master's perfect design for women included this longing for unconditional love, enjoyed and expressed through relationships.

This longing for relationship carries the blessing of enabling us to relate to God and others in a beautiful way, but it also carries a vulnerability. The enemy likes to lie and twist our need for love into something destructive. For every good gift God has for us, Satan has a counterfeit. The world offers us a lot of false love and false ways of getting love. Often we are tempted to wear masks to get people to love us. We try to be what we think they want us to be instead of just being the amazing person God created us to be. Maybe you had a parent, coach, or teacher who made you feel like love was attached to your performance. If you did well and achieved, they were proud of you and gave you affection. If you failed, they communicated that you were a disappointment. Perhaps you had a family member who made you feel like a burden, or a friend who made you feel like you didn't belong.

I have a dear friend who felt unloved as early as she can remember because she was born with some physical defects and had to have many surgeries as a child. Instead of feeling loved by her family, she felt like a bother to them. Her parents are good people and truly do love her, but it was easier for her to believe the lie that she was unlovable than it was to believe she was loved. If you met her, you'd think she's beautiful and successful on the outside, yet she still feels unloved on the inside. Maybe you can relate.

Who or what circumstances make you feel unloved?

Ask the Holy Spirit to show you when you first started to believe that lie. When did Satan get that foothold in your life?

Anything that makes you feel unworthy of love is a lie from the enemy. When Satan whispers these lies in your ear, reject the words in Jesus' name. Turn your focus to listening to Jesus and ask Him to prevent Satan's lies from having any power over you.

Any boy who claims to love you and asks you to do something against God's best plan for you is lying to you. Try quoting this truth back at his lies: "God is love" (1 John 4:8). Anything that is not of God, is not love, and anything that is not pure, unconditional love is not from God.

This is how God loves: "But God showed his great love for us by sending Christ to die for us while we were still sinners" (Romans 5:8), and "See how very much our Father loves us, for he calls us his children, and that is what we are!" (1 John 3:1). Guess what! You were unlovable, and God loved you anyway! He sent His Son to die for you and to invite you to become part of His family. He chose you before you ever chose Him. Christ died for the world knowing millions of people would reject Him. We can be daughters of the King, worthy of love because of what Jesus did on the cross, and yet Satan will try to make us feel unloved and send us searching in all the wrong places for acceptance. Why are we falling for that? It's time for our feelings to bow to our faith. Try proclaiming that you are worthy because Christ is worthy! Remind yourself that God already loved you while you were unlovely. Stop exhausting yourself searching for love, and run into the arms of your Savior, who *is* Love. You will only find what you're longing for in Him.

Run to Jesus just as you are. He's waiting with open arms to accept you right where you're at. Don't worry if you've made mistakes searching for love in all the wrong places. God's love is unconditional. You can't be good enough to earn it. You don't deserve it. You can't buy it. You can only humble yourself, confess your unlovely past, and admit your need for a Savior. Accept what Jesus did for you on the cross as the only way to find true love:

> God showed how much he loved us by sending his one and only Son into the world so that we might have eternal life through him. This is real love—not that we loved God, but that he loved us and sent his Son as a sacrifice to take away our sins. Dear friends, since God loved us that much, we surely ought to love each other.

1 JOHN 4:9-11

Merciful Savior,

*Thank You for being Love. It's who You are.
Wow! That's all I need to know. It makes me feel
so secure. Your love is everywhere. Creation shouts
Your name through beautiful sunsets, blooming
flowers, the oceans, and their breeze. It reminds me
of Your faithfulness. You are everywhere I look.
My heart is excited for every day and every new
moment I have to discover Your love.*

*Love is what held You on the cross. I can't begin
to grasp or comprehend how big and wide and
deep Your love is. Reveal Your love to me today in
new ways and help me show Your love to others.
I lift up my hands and shout, "Holy, holy, holy,"
for You are worthy of all my praise!*

We can't see God with our eyes, but we can "see" Him through how He answers our prayers. We can feel God's love through His Word, through singing praise songs, through enjoying creation, through godly friends who encourage us. God chose you and loved you before you were born. He hand-picked you. God does not make mistakes. You are an original, one of a kind, hand-crafted by Him to love and be loved. Go spread His love today!

Think of one person who is feeling unloved right now. How could you show that person love? This is what you were made for! Go love as Christ loved!

When I feel unprepared . . . God is my GUIDE

Do you ever feel worried that you might make one wrong decision that could mess up the rest of your life? Like, what if you choose the wrong college and miss meeting your soul mate? Or, what if you choose the wrong career and miss the purpose you were destined to fulfill? In the next few years, you will have many new experiences like deciding where to go to school, filling out your first job application, deciding what career to pursue, and choosing who to date or not to date. Sometimes you will feel excited to have these new freedoms and other times you might feel unprepared to make these choices.

"Adulting" is both exciting and scary! If you feel unprepared for the rest of your life, don't worry. You don't have to have it all figured out because God is your guide. Pursuing God is more important than knowing the plan. God is writing your story, and you can trust Him one day at a time.

If you are pursuing God and obeying His Word, you won't miss the best plans He has for you. The problem comes when we make sinful choices that go against God's Word and take us on detours off God's path. As soon as we confess our sin, God is faithful and just to forgive us and to cleanse us (1 John 1:9). But that doesn't mean we won't experience the pain and consequences of our sin. I love that the Bible describes so many imperfect people whose bad choices were redeemed by God, who still used them for His glory. That means God will take the good, the bad, and the ugly of your life and redeem you too. He will guide you to where He wants you to go and get you back on the right path. The key is to know His voice and follow Him. The more time you spend with God, the more you will know His voice. Here's a clear promise: "Trust in the LORD with all your heart; do not depend on your own understanding. Seek his will in all you do, and he will show you which path to take" (Proverbs 3:5–6).

Father God,

You are my Guide. Draw me so close to You that I can feel Your heartbeat. I want to be in step with You every moment of the day. I don't want to miss one plan You have for me. Help me to hear Your voice above every other voice. Thank You that I don't have to worry because, when I am following You, I am on the right path.

You have plans to prosper me and not to harm me. My future and my destiny are both in Your hands. I can't wait to see what doors You open today. When I am holding Your hand—that's when miracles happen. I can't wait! I raise my hands in complete submission and dependence on You today.

After our accident, my family was tempted at times to ask the *What Ifs*: What if I had ridden in a different car with my friends and never been injured? What if we had ordered pizza from Domino's and not gone to Kentucky Fried Chicken and not been on the same road as the drunk driver? What if we had not gone to church that night and stayed safely at home?

The *What Ifs* will drive you crazy. They imply that somehow either you or God made a mistake. We had to lay down our *What Ifs* in exchange for trust, trust that God knew before the foundation of the world exactly what was going to happen. He allowed us to be on the right road at the right time with that drunk driver to give us a new purpose, His purpose. We can make plans, but God's purposes will always prevail. In God's sovereignty, He knew through the tragedy of the car wreck, our faith would come out stronger and He would birth a ministry that would take the gospel all over the world.

One of the stories that brings me the most confidence when I feel unprepared for my future is Paul's shipwreck. (I know it sounds crazy that a wreck could bring anyone comfort.) Paul was on his way to Rome. He was certain God had a great work for him to do in that city, and he had waited for more than two years in prison for a chance to get there. Finally, when God seemed to open the doors for Paul to sail to Rome, Paul was shipwrecked and stuck on a tiny, insignificant island called Malta.

At the time, it must have felt like a disastrous mistake, but Paul ended up healing their sick and telling the people in Malta about Jesus (Acts 28). He didn't plan to go there, but God guided him safely through a storm to the exact place where He wanted Paul to fulfill His purpose. If God could use a shipwreck to get Paul where he needed to go, God can intervene to get you to the right place!

Dear Good Shepherd,

*Thank You for the honor I have in trusting in You.
I'm reminded in Scripture of Your faithfulness.
I love how You shipwrecked Paul because
You wanted him to witness and minister to
a people who hadn't yet heard the gospel
and to spread the gospel.*

*Please help me to know You are present with me
in every situation. I want to view everything I go
through in life as an opportunity and a platform to
share the hope found in You, Jesus. It's an honor to
go for You. Fill me with Your courage. Holy Spirit,
I know You will lead, guide, and direct me every step
of the way. You will even carry me on the hard days.*

Take comfort in knowing that every day of your life was already written in God's master plan before one of them ever came to be. He wants you to fulfill His purpose even more than you do. He will get you where you need to go. He can work through any circumstance to get you to the right place at the right time.

Remember when you feel unprepared, God has already had your life prepared in advance from the beginning of time: "For we are God's handiwork, created in Christ

Jesus to do good works, which God prepared in advance for us to do" (Ephesians 2:10 NIV). Worry less about being prepared for your future and focus more on getting close to the One who has been preparing your future long before you were born: "You saw me before I was born. Every day of my life was recorded in your book. Every moment was laid out before a single day had passed" (Psalm 139:16).

All-Knowing and All-Powerful Father,

Thank You for the confidence I have in You.
Daddy, I run to You this day. I love that even before
I was born, You had already prepared good works
for me to do. Even when I don't feel good enough
or smart enough, You will equip me. Help me never
to shrink back, but to rise up and accomplish the
impossible for You. I can't wait to see where You
take me. Jesus, I want to walk on water with You!

Every morning when I wake up, the first thing I do is land on my knees. I pray this simple prayer: "Jesus, I don't want to miss one plan You have for me today! Show me what You have prepared for me to do today." Then I get up and face my day in the confidence that whatever interruptions or surprises come my way, they are just another part of God's purpose for me!

Would you be willing to try something new? Before you reach for your cellphone in the morning, land on your knees, and pray that simple prayer: "God, I don't want to miss one plan You have for me today!" God is already working out His purposes for you; this simple action just might help you be more aware that He is actually moving mountains for you!

Pray right now, and commit to praying first thing in the morning, "Lord, I don't want to miss one plan You have for me today!"

When I feel unworthy . . . God is my SAVIOR

One of the best things about traveling and telling my story is that I get to hear other girls' stories. Of all the thousands of girls I meet all over the world, the one word that seems to pop up over and over again is *unworthy*. In fact, I cannot remember a single time that I spoke somewhere and did not meet at least one girl who felt unworthy.

If you struggle with feeling unworthy, you're in a great place! Did you know that feeling unworthy creates a path for Jesus? The gospel begins with us being unworthy. In fact, you can't be rescued until you acknowledge that you'll never be worth anything on your own. We were all born unworthy because of sin that separates us from

God and leads to death. There is nothing you can do to make yourself right in God's eyes. Christianity is the belief that you are saved not by your own worth but by faith alone in Jesus.

Every other world religion focuses on you becoming worthy or good enough to deserve heaven. These religious might contain elements of truth, but when you look closely, their primary focus is on what humans can do instead of on what Jesus has done. It's been said that Christianity is the only religion where you can be "bad" and get into heaven. No wonder people are attracted to it. Salvation through Jesus has nothing to do with you trying to work your way to where God is; it's about God coming down to where you are. Ephesians 2:8–9 explains, "God saved you by his grace when you believed. And you can't take credit for this; it is a gift from God. Salvation is not a reward for the good things we have done, so none of us can boast about it."

We can't begin to fathom what it feels like to be "worthy" —worth is part of God's being. It starts with Him and is a gift only He can give. The apostle John was taken up to heaven in a vision and describes a scene where an angel was searching for someone worthy to open a scroll that would set the end of the world in motion. In all of heaven, out of all the saints who had arrived there and the angels who dwelt there, there was no one found worthy except One:

> Then I saw a Lamb that looked as if it had been slaughtered. . . . He stepped forward and took the scroll from the right hand of the one sitting on the throne. And when he took the scroll. . . . they sang a new song with these words:

> > "You are worthy to take the scroll
> >   and break its seals and open it.
> > For you were slaughtered, and your blood
> >   has ransomed people for God
> >   from every tribe and language and
> >   people and nation. . . ."
> > And you have caused them to become
> >   a Kingdom of priests for our God.
> >   And they will reign on the earth."

> Then I looked again, and I heard the voices of thousands and millions of angels around the throne. . . . And they sang in a mighty chorus:

"Worthy is the Lamb who was
slaughtered—
to receive power and riches
and wisdom and strength
and honor and glory and blessing."

And then I heard every creature in heaven
and on earth and under the earth and in
the sea. They sang:

"Blessing and honor and glory and power
belong to the one sitting on the throne
and to the Lamb forever and ever."

REVELATION 5:6–13

Dear Lamb of God,
who takes away the sins of the world,

You, the King of kings, are worthy—worthy of
our praise, worthy to be magnified. You put meaning
to those words. Worthiness is anchored in who
You are alone. I love that! We praise You, Worthy
One, for all You are and all You have done. I believe
the word worthy shouts Your name.

Jesus, I can't even begin to fathom what You did to humble Yourself and come to earth. The God of the universe who is everywhere at once took on human form—what an act of grace. Then, You went to the cross and suffered an excruciating death so brutal it hurts me to even mention it. Then You overcame death because You are worthy. You are the rightful Heir. You are King. It's not even a question; it's a fact we need to embrace. We need to shout Your worthiness. We need to join the seraphim in God's throne room and shout, "Holy, holy, holy!" Worthy One, You are more than enough for me.

Jesus proved He was worthy by living a sinless life in a human body. He endured temptation and pain just like we experience, but He was the only human who never sinned. Then He conquered death and rose again, proving He was more than human: He was God. He is the only one who can make me feel worthy. He transfers His righteousness to me when I confess my sins and trust Him as my Savior. Until you surrender to Jesus, you will never stop feeling unworthy.

If you have never known God as your Savior, He made a way to transfer His worth to you. First, *admit you are a sinner and repent:* "We are all infected and impure with sin. When we display our righteous deeds, they are nothing but filthy rags" (Isaiah 64:6). To repent is more than just feeling sorry for your sins. It means changing your behavior and turning away from your sin to follow Jesus. Then, *believe Jesus died for your sins:* "For this is how God loved the world: He gave his one and only Son, so that everyone who believes in him will not perish but have eternal life" (John 3:16). Finally, *confess you need Jesus' death and resurrection to make you worthy of salvation:* "If you openly declare that Jesus is Lord and believe in your heart that God raised him from the dead, you will be saved" (Romans 10:9).

When I feel unworthy of God's love, I only have to look to the cross. Jesus and His sacrifice on the cross make me worthy. God loved us so much that He made a way for us to become worthy through the shed blood of His Son. He is our hope. He is our worth. I can stand on it and trust Him.

 Write a prayer thanking and praising God that you are worthy because of Him and what He did for you on the cross:

When I feel unknown . . .
God is ALL-KNOWING

Over the next few years, you will probably step into new, exciting seasons. The possibilities are so varied and the opportunities will be great, but chances are, the surroundings will sometimes be brand-new. Maybe you'll start a new school, move to a new town to attend college, get your first job, or try a new extracurricular activity. You and I both know that you are amazing, but it's possible you might find yourself in a new situation where people don't know everything about you. Maybe at times *you* won't know everything about you because so much around you is changing. You may wrestle with who you want to be and what you should be doing right now.

If you ever find yourself in a situation where not everyone knows your name or your claim to fame, take comfort in the truth that your heavenly Daddy knows everything about everything, which means He knows everything about you! He knows how many hairs are on your head. He knows the wounds hidden deep in your heart. He knows every thought in your head and every breath you take. God even knows what you are going to say before you decide to say it:

> You see me when I travel
> and when I rest at home.
> You know everything I do.
> You know what I am going to say
> even before I say it, Lord.

PSALM 139:3-4

When you feel unknown or tempted to wear masks to fit into a new crowd, remember there is a Friend who knows every detail about you and loves you just the way you are. This gives me such freedom because I can be real and honest with God. Since He knows what I'm thinking, I don't have to cover up and act fine when I'm struggling. I can tell God when I'm angry or scared or frustrated because He already knows.

What situations are you in right now where you feel unknown?

 Are you tempted to wear any masks to fit in?

Tell God what you are struggling with. Ask Him to help you be free to be you. Try writing a prayer to Him expressing these thoughts:

Maybe you have a different struggle. Maybe you over-compensate with confidence or trying to achieve more things to make yourself known. Maybe you need to be set free from the pressure of trying to make your name famous. Pure joy and fulfillment comes when we make Jesus famous and make His name known to everyone we meet. We were not made for glory. We were made to reflect any praise or glory we receive onto our Creator: "In the same way, let your good deeds shine out for all to see, so that everyone will praise your heavenly Father" (Matthew 5:16).

When we strive for own glory or hold on to it for too long, it has a tendency to ruin us. Just look at the lives and relationships of people in Hollywood. Have you ever wondered why so many childhood stars go bad? We weren't meant to hold on to all that fame. God gives fame and favor for us to use it to point people to Him.

What if we took all the time and energy we spend trying to make ourselves known and invested it in getting to know who God is? If you really want to know who you are or what version of yourself you should be, get to know the One who knows everything about you. The closer you get to God, the more you'll understand who He is and who you were designed to be. Jesus explained, "Those who accept my commandments and obey them are the ones who love me. And because they love me, my Father will love them. And I will love them and reveal myself to each of them" (John 14:21).

God sees from the beginning to the end. He is the Beginning and the End. He has always existed, even before time, and long before you were born. If you want to know who you are and you want others to really know you, get to know the One who knows every hair on your head. You are a thread in His quilt, one small but important piece in His master puzzle. He is working all things for His glory and for His eternal kingdom that will never end.

Make Him known and you too will be known by the only One who really matters.

Father,

Please reveal to me my true identity, who I am in Your eyes. I want to learn who I am so I can be a better servant, a better follower, a better disciple of the most high King. WOW! It's such an honor.

Thank You that You see me and accept me just as I am. You see my future and my dreams. But Lord, I want to flip-flop my perspective and see Your dreams. I know Your dreams have eternity in mind. Your dreams are bigger than anything I could ever imagine!

Lord Jesus,

I want to walk on water with You. I know that is when miracles happen. That's when things change for eternity, when I put my faith and trust in You, in the almighty name of Jesus.

Holy Spirit,

I want to seek You and find You with all my heart. Please guide me every step of the way. I want to make my mark on the world by putting my trust in You. Even though I can't see the future, I know You hold my future. I can't wait to see what You will do through me today!

Dear Sweet Sister,

I'm so proud of you and so is the King of kings! You make Him smile!

Even though our study is coming to an end, I pray it won't stop here, but that you would continue to embrace the new you and see yourself every day a little more through the eyes of your heavenly Daddy. He is always there for you, to comfort you and to guide you. He wants you to run to Him and share your dreams and your disappointments.

I pray you will allow God to capture your whole heart. Choose to go on an adventure with Him every single day. He is your lifelong companion!

Beyond Priceless has given you a model of how to open God's Word and talk back and forth to God about what you are reading. God wants to be your Best Friend. He wants to help you understand His Word and longs to reveal more truth to you. God will never abandon you. Even when life gets hard, you can trust Him with your future. He is a good, good Father. His plans for your life are far greater than anything you could imagine.

Jeremiah 29:11–13 says, "For I know the plans I have for you," says the LORD. "They are plans for good and not for disaster, to give you a future and a hope. . . . when you pray, I will listen. If you look for me wholeheartedly, you will find me."

Don't ever give up! God is *more* than enough to meet your every need. He can't wait to reveal more of Himself to you!

Always remember that you are never alone. God is holding your hand. He is your Redeemer, your Healer, your Defender, your Protector, your Provider, and the Lover of Your Soul.

I'm believing your best days are yet to come.

Love,

Jen

A Note and Prayer from Jen

Dear Heavenly Daddy,

*Please cradle my sweet sister in Your everlasting
arms today and whisper hope to her heart.
Her journey isn't done, Lord. This is just the start!
I pray that she would grab on to the hem of
Your garment and go where You lead.*

*Help her to view this day with expectation,
abundance, and potential. Today hasn't been
written. You are the author of her story. You can't
wait to take her to places she never dreamed
possible. Fill her with strength to go on the
adventure with You. Bless her today with Your joy
and peace. I pray she will experience more
of You each day. Thank You for being
her Almighty, Great I AM! Woohoo!*

*Lord, You are infinitely more than our
human minds can even fathom.*

You are Beyond Priceless!

Amen!

ACKNOWLEDGMENTS

There aren't enough words to express how grateful I am for my dad, Andy, who loves me unconditionally. He is so patient with all of my disabilities and memory problems. My dad believes in me and teaches me never to give up.

A huge thank you to my aunt Christy Murphy for helping my mom and me write this book. She listens to God's voice and has amazing wisdom and insight. Our brainstorming sessions always include a few laughs, along with lots of coffee and ice cream.

YOUR FEELINGS AREN'T A BAD THING.

They are a gift from God to make space in your heart for more of I

In this 30-day devotional for teen girls, Jen Barrick, with the help
of her mom, Linda Barrick, compiled her own real-life prayers
with passages from Psalms in order to speak directly to the heart o
young women. It will teach teens how to cultivate a deep, emotior
relationship with the God who loves them.

978-0-8024-1871-5 l also available as an eBook

MOODY
Publishers®

From the Word to Life®